The Ultimate Self-Teaching Method!

BEGINNER'S PACK

Play Trumpet Today!

A Complete Guide to the Basics

To access audio and video visit:
www.halleonard.com/mylibrary

Enter Code
7020-2183-8324-1476

ISBN 978-1-5400-5243-8

Visit Hal Leonard Online at
www.halleonard.com

Contact us:
Hal Leonard
7777 West Bluemound Road
Milwaukee, WI 53213
Email: info@halleonard.com

In Europe, contact:
Hal Leonard Europe Limited
42 Wigmore Street
Marylebone, London, W1U 2RN
Email: info@halleonardeurope.com

In Australia, contact:
Hal Leonard Australia Pty. Ltd.
4 Lentara Court
Cheltenham, Victoria, 3192 Australia
Email: info@halleonard.com.au

Contents

Introduction

Welcome to *Play Trumpet Today!*—the method designed to prepare you for any style of trumpet playing, from rock to blues to jazz to classical. Whatever your taste in music, *Play Trumpet Today!* will give you the start you need.

About the Audio & Video

It's easy and fun to play trumpet, and the accompanying audio will make your learning even more enjoyable, as we take you step by step through each lesson and play each song along with a full band. Much as a real lesson, the best way to learn this material is to read and practice a while first on your own, then listen to the audio. With *Play Trumpet Today!*, you can learn at your own pace. If there is ever something that you don't quite understand the first time through, go back to the audio and listen again. Every musical track has been given a track number, so if you want to practice a song again, you can find it right away.

Some topics in the book include video lessons, so you can see and hear the material being taught. Audio and video are indicated with icons.

The Basics

The Parts of the Trumpet

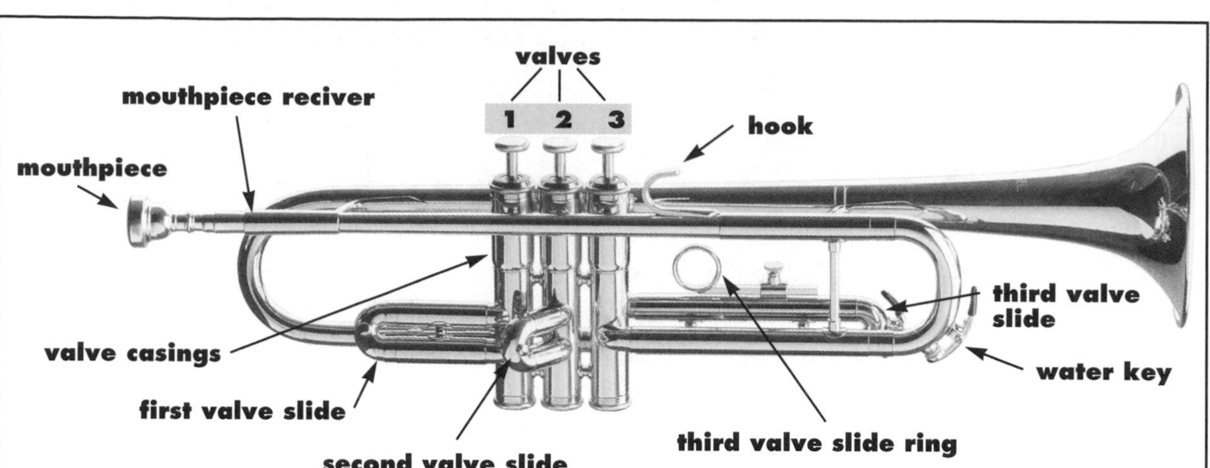

Posture

Whether sitting on the edge of your chair or standing, you should always keep your:

- Spine straight and tall,
- Shoulders back and relaxed, and
- Feet flat on the floor.

Breathing & Air Stream

Breathing is a natural thing we all do constantly, but you must control your breathing while playing the trumpet. To discover the correct air stream to play your trumpet:

- Place the palm of your hand near your mouth.
- Inhale deeply through the corners of your mouth, keeping your shoulders steady. Your waist should expand like a balloon.
- Whisper "tah" as you gradually exhale a stream of air into your palm.

The air you feel is the air stream. It produces sound through the instrument. Your tongue is like a faucet or valve that releases or stops the air stream.

Your First Tone 

Your mouth's position on the instrument is called the embouchure (*ahm' bah shure*). Developing a good embouchure takes time and effort, so carefully follow these beginning steps:

- Moisten your lips and bring them together as if saying the letter "m."
- Relax your jaw, separating your upper and lower teeth.
- Form a slightly puckered smile to firm the corners of your mouth.
- Direct a full air stream through the center of your lips, creating a buzz. (You should buzz frequently without your mouthpiece.)
- While forming your "buzzing" embouchure, center the mouthpiece on your lips.
- Take in a full breath through the corners of your mouth and start your buzz with the syllable "tah." Your tongue will act like a valve, opening up the stream of air. Buzz through the center of your lips and try to keep the sound steady and even. This will probably feel very strange and even silly to you at first, but this buzzing is the fundamental sound of all brass instruments.

Reading Music 

Musical sounds are indicated by symbols called **notes** written on a **staff**. Notes come in several forms, but every note indicates **pitch** and **rhythm**.

The Staff

Music Staff

The **music staff** has 5 lines and 4 spaces where notes and rests are written.

Ledger Lines

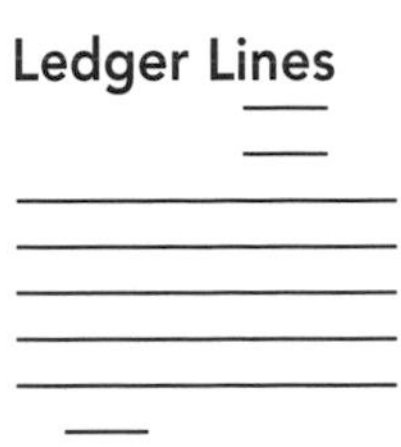

Ledger lines extend the music staff. Notes on ledger lines can be above or below the staff.

Measures & Bar Lines

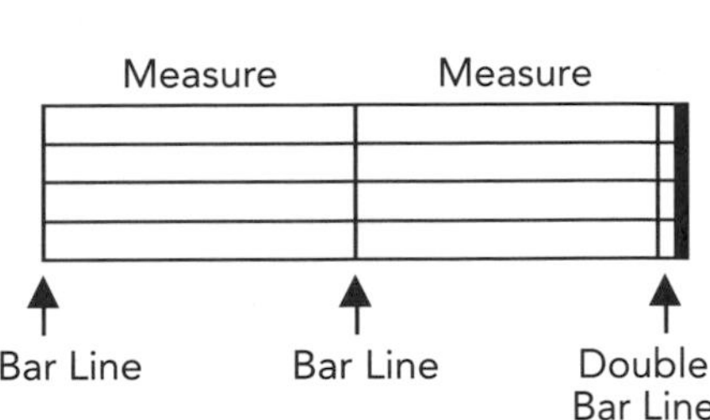

Bar lines divide the music staff into **measures.** The **Double Bar** indicates the end of a piece of music.

Treble Clef (G Clef) indicates the position of note names on a music staff: Second line is G.

Time Signature indicates how many beats per measure and what kind of note gets one beat.

= **4 beats** per measure
= **Quarter note** gets one beat

Pitch

Pitch (the highness or lowness of a note) is indicated by the horizontal placement of the note on the staff. Notes higher on the staff are higher in pitch; notes lower on the staff are lower in pitch. To name the pitches, we use the first seven letters of the alphabet: A, B, C, D, E, F, and G. The **treble clef** (𝄞) assigns a particular pitch name to each line and space on the staff, centered around the pitch G, located on the second line of the staff. Music for the trumpet is always written in the treble clef. (Some instruments may make use of other clefs, which make the lines and spaces represent different pitches.)

Note Names

Each note is on a line or space of the staff. These note names are indicated by the Treble Clef.

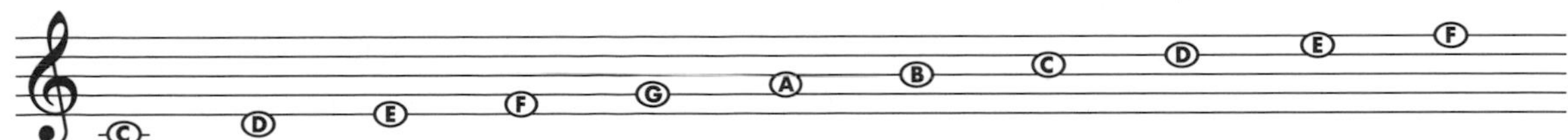

Sharps, Flats, and Naturals

These musical symbols are called accidentals which raise or lower the pitch of a note.

Sharp ♯ raises the note and remains in effect for the entire measure.

Flat ♭ lowers the note and remains in effect for the entire measure.

Natural ♮ cancels a flat (♭) or sharp (♯) and remains in effect for the entire measure.

Rhythm

Rhythm refers to how long, or for how many **beats** a note lasts. The beat is the pulse of music, and like your heartbeat it usually remains very steady. To help keep track of the beats in a piece of music, the staff is divided into **measures**. The **time signature** (numbers such as $\frac{4}{4}$ or $\frac{6}{8}$ at the beginning of the staff) indicates how many beats you will find in each measure. Counting the beats or tapping your foot can help to maintain a steady beat. Tap your foot down on each beat and up on each "&."

$\frac{4}{4}$ Time

Count:	1	&	2	&	3	&	4	&
Tap:	↓	↑	↓	↑	↓	↑	↓	↑

$\frac{4}{4}$ is probably the most common time signature. The **top number** tells you how many beats are in each measure; the **bottom number** tells you what kind of note receives one beat. In $\frac{4}{4}$ time there are four beats in the measure and a **quarter note** (♩ or 𝅘𝅥) equals one beat.

4 = **4 beats** per measure
4 = **Quarter note** gets one beat

Assembling Your Trumpet 

- Hold the trumpet with your left hand. Your thumb and your fingers should grasp the instrument around the valve casings. Put your left ring finger inside the third valve slide ring. (Refer to the picture under "The Parts of the Trumpet.")
- Hold the mouthpiece at the wide end with your right hand. Gently twist the mouthpiece into the mouthpiece receiver. Never pound the mouthpiece in. It can get stuck, and you will need special equipment (called a "mouthpiece puller") to get it out without damaging your trumpet.

How to Hold Your Trumpet

- Arch your right hand to form a backwards "C." Rest your right thumb alongside the first valve casing under the straight tube that leads to the mouthpiece. Your fingers will rest on the three valves, with your little finger resting on the top of the hook. Don't try to support the trumpet with your right hand. The left hand will hold the weight of the instrument and the right hand will merely help balance it.
- Always sit or stand tall when playing. Hold the trumpet as shown:

Putting Away Your Instrument 

- Blow air through the trumpet while opening the water key(s) to empty any condensation from the instrument.
- Remove the mouthpiece and put it in the appropriate place in your case. Once a week, wash the mouthpiece with warm tap water and dry thoroughly.
- Wipe off your trumpet with a clean, soft cloth. Return the instrument to its case.
- Occasionally your slides will need greasing. Obtain special slide grease from your music dealer.
- You should oil your valves regularly. Only use specially-made valve oil, which should be available from your musical instrument dealer. To oil your trumpet valves:
    1.) Unscrew the valve at the top of the valve casing and lift the valve half-way out.
    2.) Apply a few drops of valve oil to the exposed valve.
    3.) Carefully return the valve into its casing. It will only fit one way, and the top of the valve should easily screw back into place once it is properly inserted.

Lesson 1

Track 1

The First Note: G

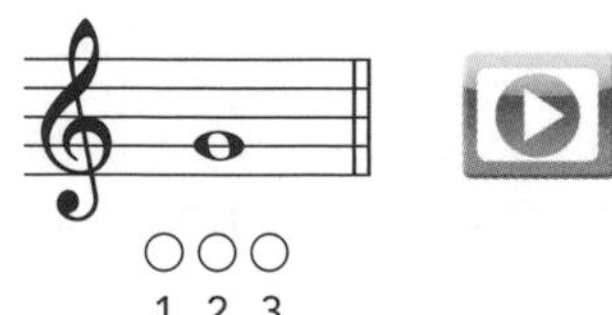

G is played "open" that is, with no valves pressed. Rest your fingers on the valves, relaxed and curved. Many different notes can be played open on the trumpet, so match your pitch to the track.

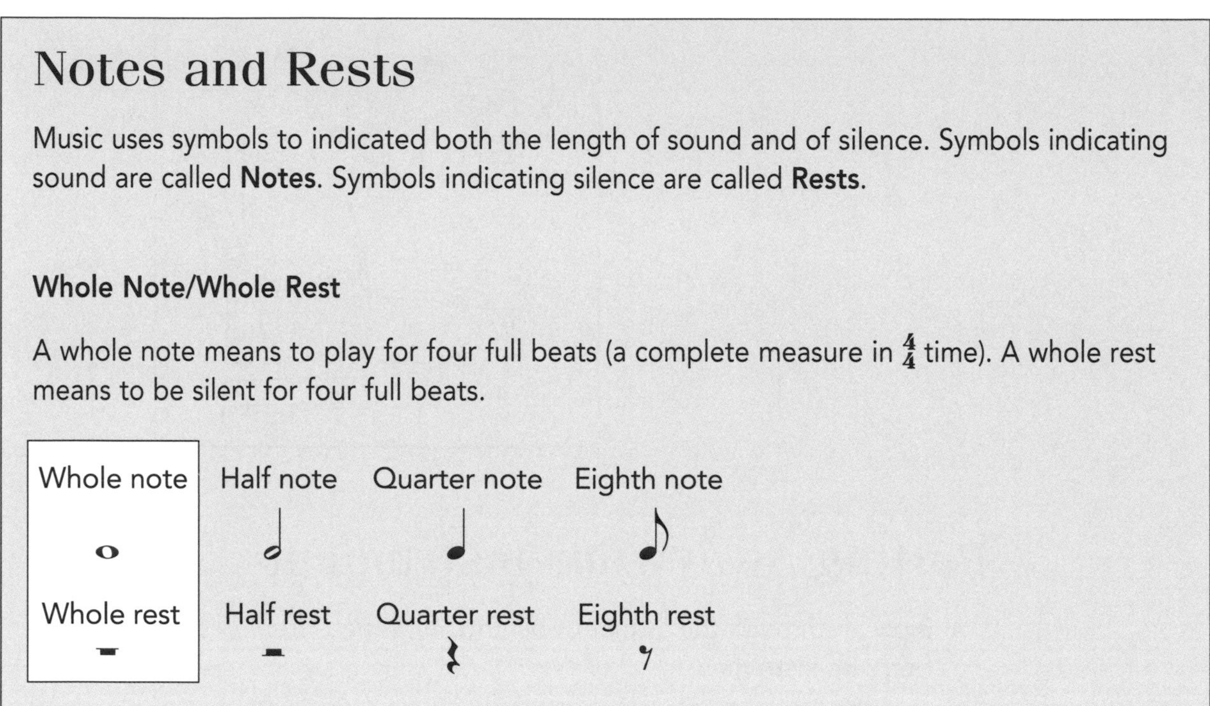

Notes and Rests

Music uses symbols to indicated both the length of sound and of silence. Symbols indicating sound are called **Notes**. Symbols indicating silence are called **Rests**.

Whole Note/Whole Rest

A whole note means to play for four full beats (a complete measure in $\frac{4}{4}$ time). A whole rest means to be silent for four full beats.

Listen to recorded track, then play along. Try to match the sound on the recording.

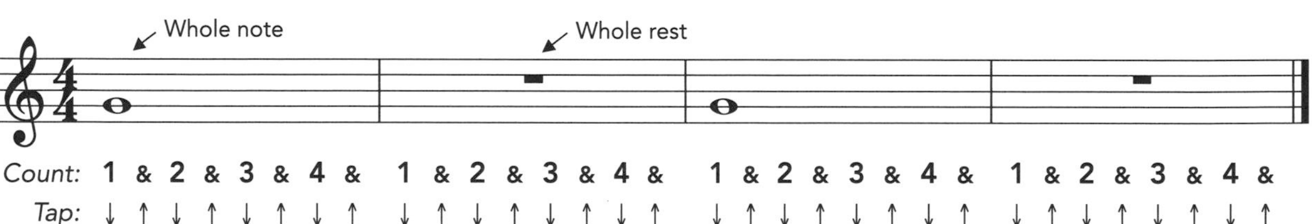

Track 2

Count and Play

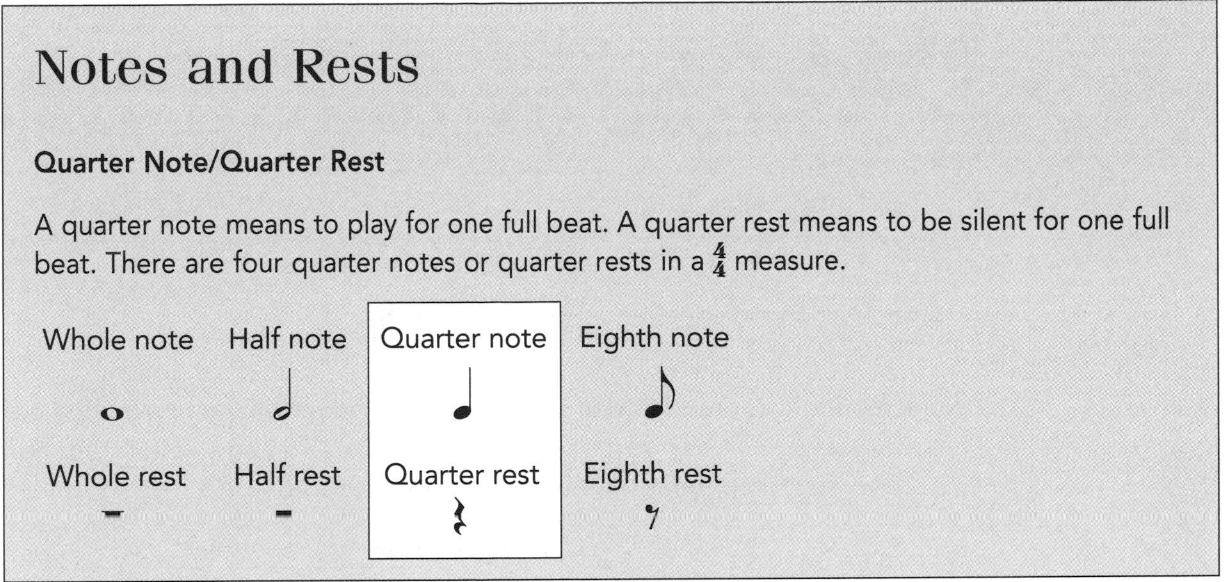

Notes and Rests

Quarter Note/Quarter Rest

A quarter note means to play for one full beat. A quarter rest means to be silent for one full beat. There are four quarter notes or quarter rests in a $\frac{4}{4}$ measure.

Each note should begin with a quick "tu" to help separate it from the others.

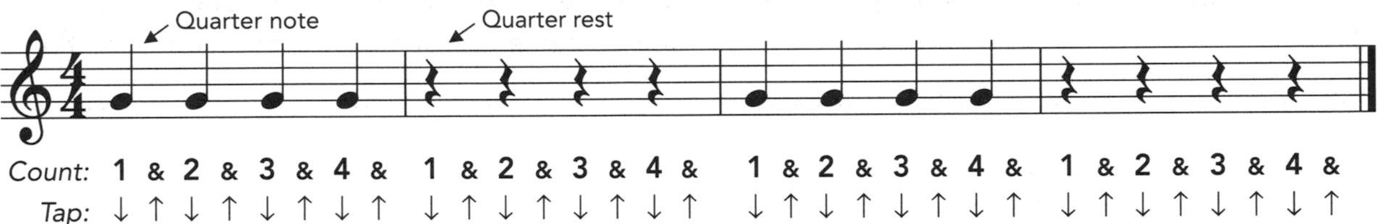

Don't just let the audio play on. Repeat each exercise until you feel comfortable playing it by yourself and with the recording.

Track 3

A New Note: F

Look for the fingering diagram under each new note. Press down the valves that are colored in. F is played with the 1st valve. Practicing long tones like this will help to develop your sound and your breath control, so don't just move on to the next exercise. Repeat each one several times.

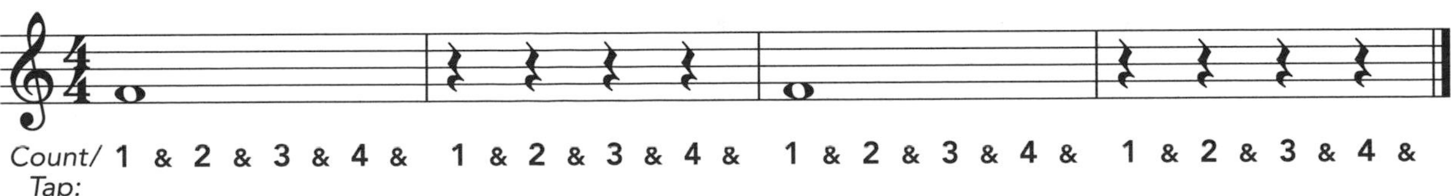

Two's A Team

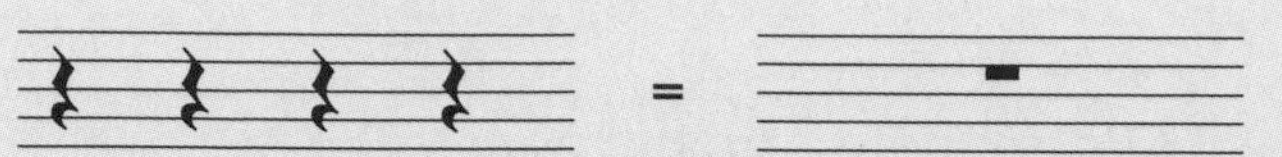

Remember: Rests are silence in music where you play nothing at all. Rests are like notes in that they have their own rhythmic values, instructing you how long (or for how many beats) to pause. Here, four beats of rest can be simplified as a whole rest.

A New Note: E

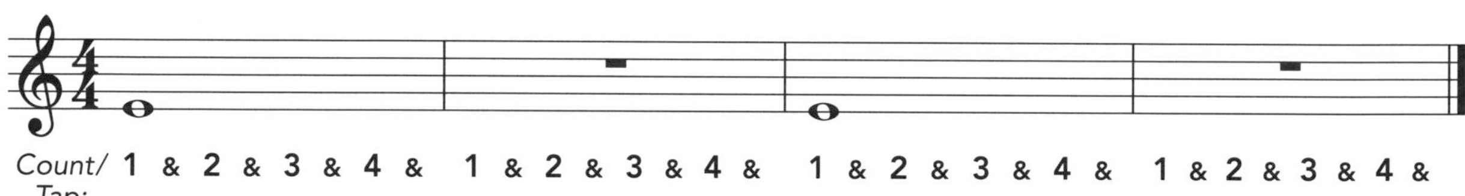

Keeping Time

To keep a steady tempo, try tapping your foot and counting along with each song. In $\frac{4}{4}$ time, tap your foot four times in each measure and count, "1 & 2 & 3 & 4 &." Your foot should touch the floor on the number and come up on the "&." Each number and each "&" should be exactly the same duration, like the ticking of a clock.

Moving On Up

If you become winded or your lips get tired, you can still practice by fingering the notes on your instrument and singing the pitches or counting the rhythm out loud.

Track 7

A New Note: D

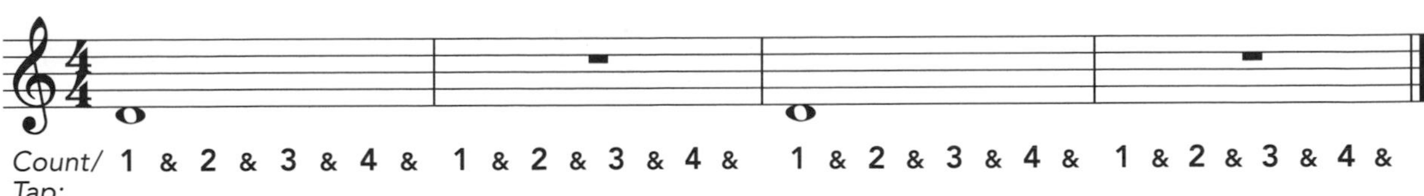

Track 8

Four By Four

Repeat Signs

Repeat signs [repeat sign symbol] tell you to repeat everything between them. If only the sign on the right appears (:‖), repeat from the beginning of the piece.

Track 9

A New Note: C

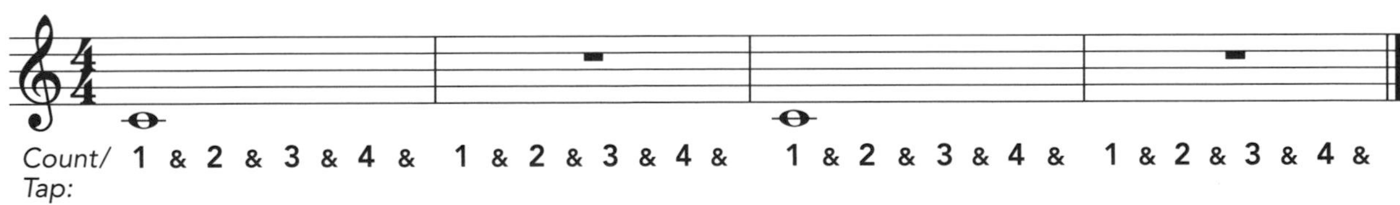

Track 10

The Fab Five

Track 11

First Flight

Keep the beat steady by silently counting or tapping while you play.

Track 12

Rolling Along

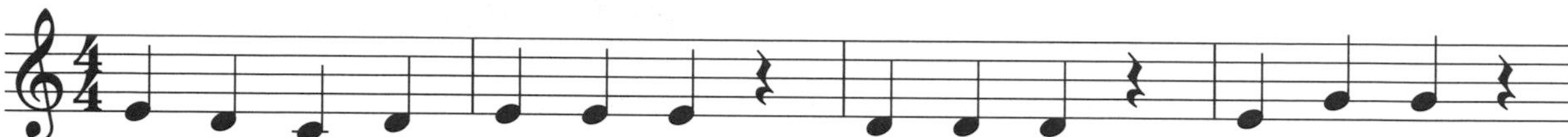

Tonguing

To start each note, whisper the syllable "tu." Keep the air stream going continuously and just flick the tip of your tongue against the back of your upper teeth for each new note. If the notes change, be sure to move your fingers quickly so that each note will come out cleanly. When you come to a rest or the end of the song, just stop blowing. Using your tongue to stop the air will cause an abrupt and unpleasant ending of the sound.

Lesson 2

- Play long tones to warm up at the beginning of every practice session.
- Tap, count out loud and sing through each exercise with the audio before you play it.
- Play each exercise several times until you feel comfortable with it.

Track 13

Hot Cross Buns

Notes and Rests

Half Note/Half Rest

A half note means to play for two full beats. (It's equal in length to two quarter notes.) A half rest means to be silent for two beats. There are two half notes or half rests in a $\frac{4}{4}$ measure.

Whole note	Half note	Quarter note	Eighth note
Whole rest	Half rest	Quarter rest	Eighth rest

Half note

Half rest

Track 14

Go Tell Aunt Rhodie

Breath Mark

The breath mark (,) indicates a specific place to inhale. Play the proceeding note for the full length then take a deep, quick breath through your mouth.

Make certain that your cheeks don't puff out when you blow.

Track 15

The Whole Thing

Remember: a whole rest (-) indicates a whole measure of silence. Note that the whole rest hangs down from the 4th line, whereas the half rest sits on the 3rd line.

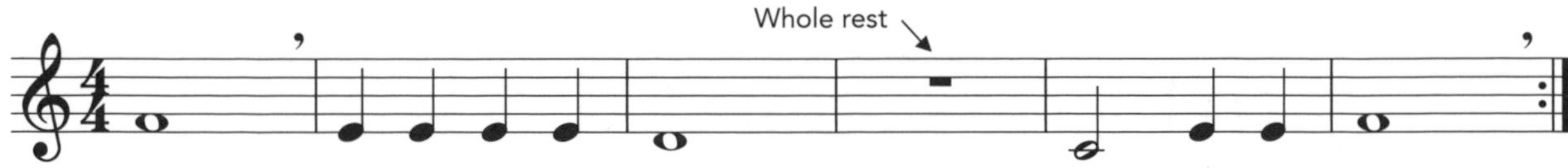

Track 16

Lightly Row

Track 17

Reaching Higher (New Note: A)

Always practice long tones on each new note.

Fermata

The fermata (𝄐) indicates that a note or rest is held somewhat longer than normal.

Au Claire De La Lune

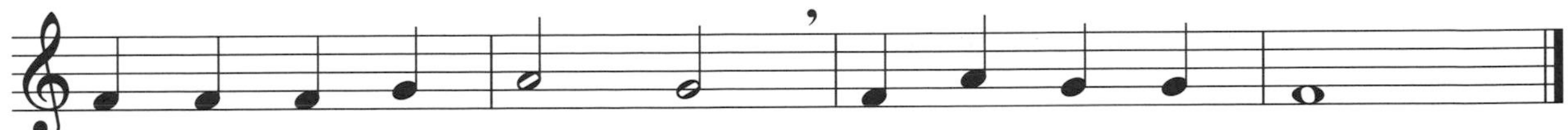

Twinkle, Twinkle Little Star

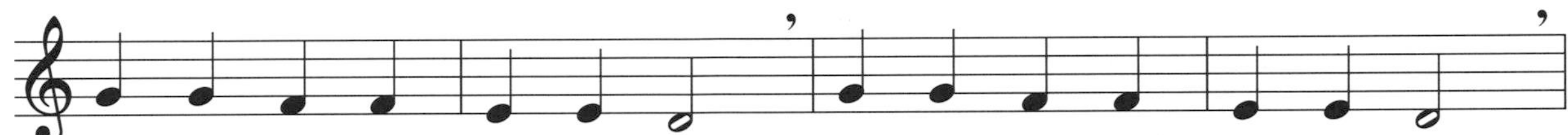

Lesson 3

Check these points so you will get the best sound from your trumpet.

- If you get a bubbling sound as you play, drain the water from the slides by pressing the water keys as you blow air (without buzzing your lips) through the trumpet. If this doesn't help, pull the slides individually and empty the water from them.
- Make certain that your cheeks don't puff out when you blow.
- Keep the center section of your lips relaxed at all times.

Track 20

Deep Pockets (New Note: B)

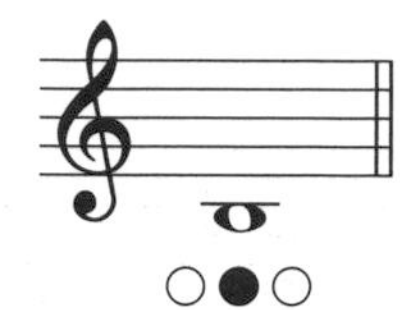

Always practice long tones on each new note.

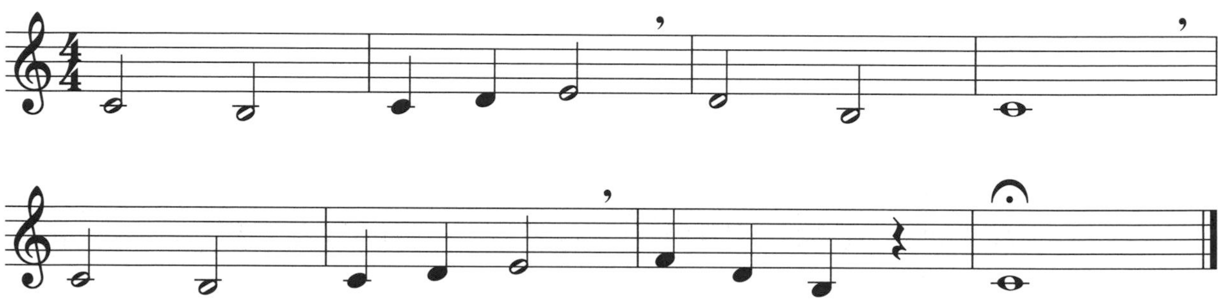

Track 21

Doodle All Day

Try to play this on your mouthpiece only before you play it on your trumpet.

Breath Support

In order to play in tune and with a full, beautiful tone, it is necessary to breathe properly and control the air as you play. Quickly take the breath in through your mouth all the way to the bottom of your lungs. Then tighten your stomach muscles and push the air quickly through the trumpet, controlling the air with your lips. Practice this by forming your lips as you do when you play and then blowing against your hand. If the air is cool, you are doing it correctly. If the air is warm, tighten the lips and make the air stream smaller. Keep the air stream moving fast at all times, especially as you begin to run out of air. Practice blowing against your hand and see how long you can keep the air going. Work to keep the air stream from beginning to end.

Now try this with your trumpet. Select a note that is comfortable to play and see how long you can hold it. Listen carefully to yourself to see if the tone gets louder or softer, changes pitch slightly, or if the quality of the tone changes. Do this a few times every time you practice, trying to hold the note a little longer each time and maintain a good sound.

Track 22

Jingle Bells

Dynamics

Dynamics refer to how loud or soft the music is. Traditionally, many musical terms (including dynamic markings) are called by their Italian names:

f	forte (*four' tay*)	loud
mf	mezzo forte (*met' zoh four' tay*)	moderately loud
p	piano (*pee ahn' oh*)	soft

Producing a louder sound requires more air, but you should use full breath support at all dynamic levels.

Track 23

My Dreydl

Pick-up Notes

Sometimes there are notes that come before the first full measure. They are called **pick-up notes**. Often, when a song begins with a pick-up measure, the note's value (in beats) is subtracted from the last measure. To play this song with a one beat pick-up, you count "1, 2, 3" and start playing on beat 4.

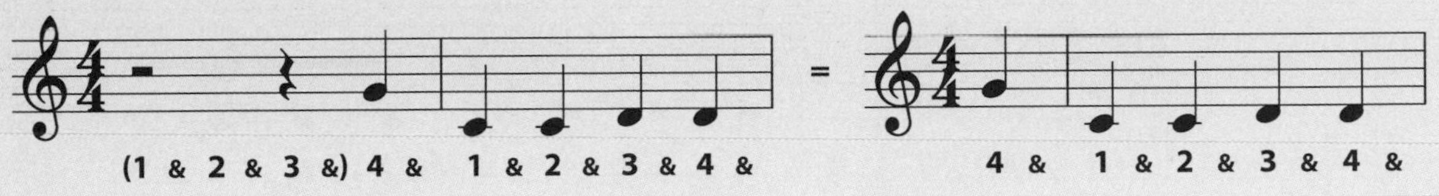

Track 24

Eighth Note Jam

Notes and Rests

Eighth Note/Eighth Rest

An eighth note is half the value of a quarter note, that is, half a beat. A eighth rest means to be silent for half a beat. There are eight eighth notes or eight eighth rests in a 4/4 measure.

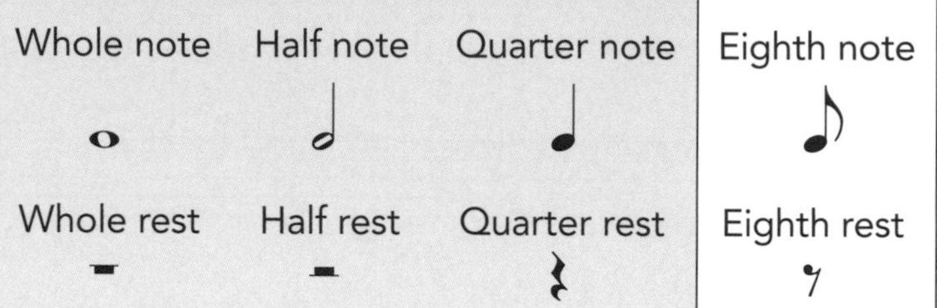

Two eighth notes = One quarter note

It is common to join two or more eighth notes with a beam (two beamed eighth notes or four beamed eighth notes). Individual eighth notes look like a quarter note with a flag on the stem (eighth note symbol or eighth note symbol).

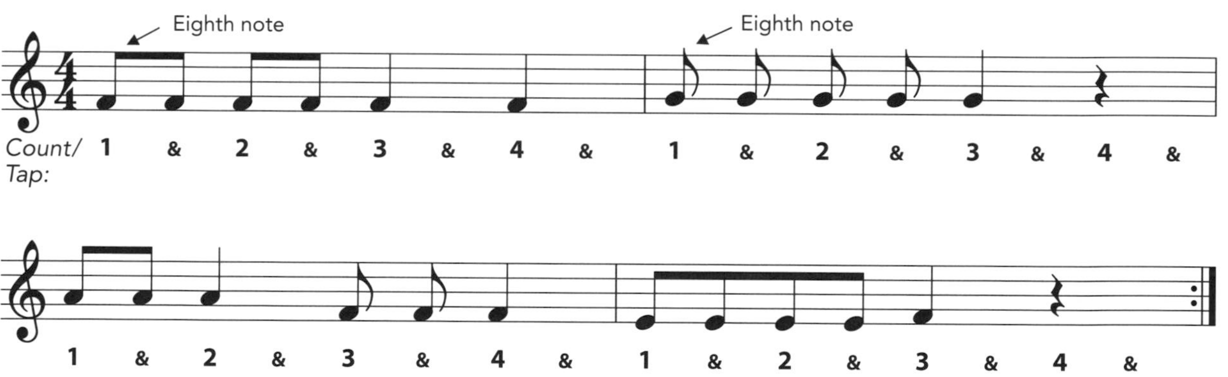

Eighth Note Counting

The first eighth note comes on "1" as your foot taps the floor. The second happens as your foot moves up on "&." The third is on "2" and the fourth is on the next "&" and so forth. Remember to count and tap in a steady and even manner, like the ticking of a clock.

Track 25

Skip To My Lou

Keep your fingertips in contact with the valve buttons.

Track 26

Oh, Susanna

Notice the pick-up notes.

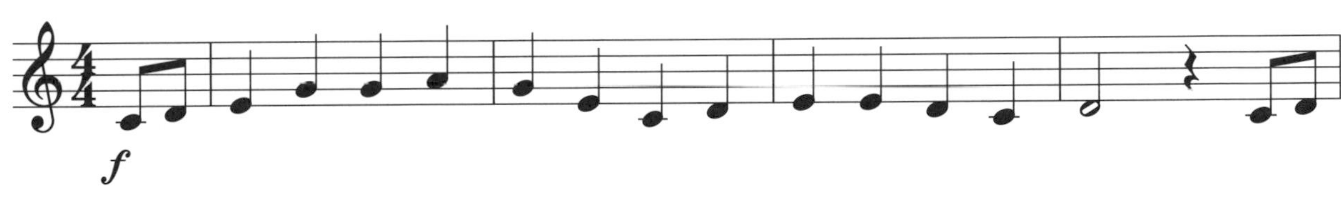

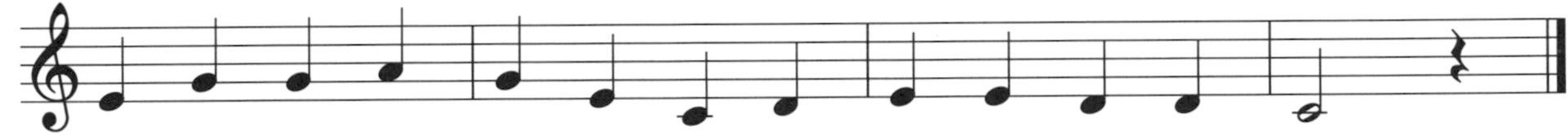

Track 27

William Tell

Good posture will improve your sound.

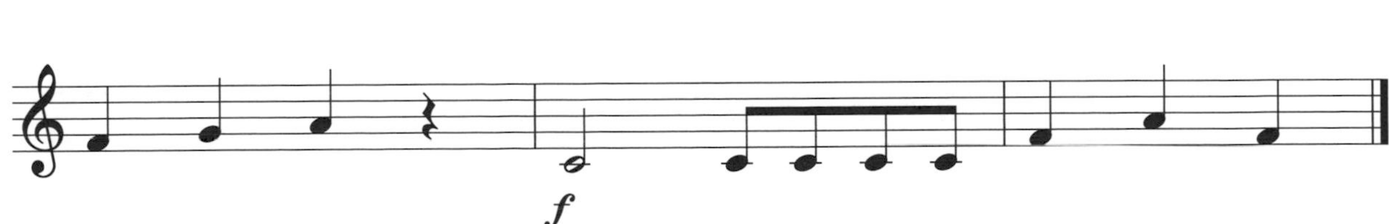

Lesson 4

- Support the trumpet with your left hand, leaving the fingers of your right hand free to move.
- Be sure to blow enough air through your trumpet for a smooth, even sound. Be careful not to blow to hard or to "blast" your tone.

Track 28

Two By Two

$\frac{2}{4}$ Time

A time signature of $\frac{2}{4}$ means that a quarter note gets one beat, but there are only two beats in a measure.

Track 29

High School Cadets March

Tempo Markings

The speed or pace of music is called **tempo**. Tempo markings are usually written above the staff. Many of these terms come from the Italian language.

Allegro	*(ah lay' grow)*	Fast tempo
Moderato	*(mah der ah' tow)*	Medium or moderate tempo
Andante	*(ahn dahn' tay)*	Slower "walking" tempo

Track 30

Hey, Ho! Nobody's Home
(New Note: A)

Octaves

Notes that have the same name but are eight notes higher or lower are called **octaves**. You already knew how to play an A, but this new A is one octave lower. Practice playing both A's one after the other like this:

The higher notes will be played more easily if you:

- With your lips, make the air stream round rather than flat.
- Move your jaw slightly forward so the high stream is directed a little higher.
- Blow the air slightly faster.

Track 31

Play The Dynamics

Dynamics

Gradual changes in volume are indicated by these symbols:

<	***Crescendo*** (gradually louder)	sometimes abbreviated *cresc.*
>	***Decrescendo*** or ***Diminuendo*** (gradually softer)	sometimes abbreviated *dim.*

Remember to keep the air stream moving fast both as you get louder by gradually using more air on the crescendo, and as you get softer by gradually using less air on the decrescendo.

Track 32

Frère Jacques

Track 33

Hard Rock Blues

Posture

Good body posture will allow you to take in a full, deep breath and control the air better as you play. Sit or stand with your spine straight and tall. Your shoulders should be back and relaxed. Think about your posture as you begin playing and check it several times while playing.

Lesson 5

Track 34

Alouette

Tie

A **tie** is a curved line connecting two notes of the same pitch. It indicates that instead of playing both notes, you play the first note and hold it for the total time value of both notes.

= 2 beats

Dot

A **dot** adds half the value of the note to which it is attached. A dotted half note (𝅗𝅥.) has a total time value of three beats:

Dotted half note (three beats)	Half note (two beats)	Quarter note (one beat)

Therefore, a dotted half note has exactly the same value as a half note tied to a quarter note. Playing track 34 again, compare this music to the previous example:

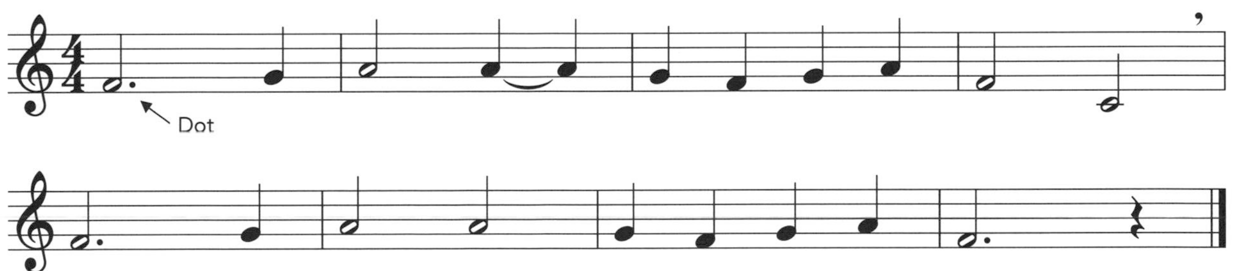

Track 35

Camptown Races

Always use a full air stream. Keep your fingers resting on top of the valves, arched naturally.

Track 36

The Nobles

Notice the tie across the bar line between the first and second measure. The G on the third beat is held through the following beats 4 and 1.

Track 37

Three Beat Jam

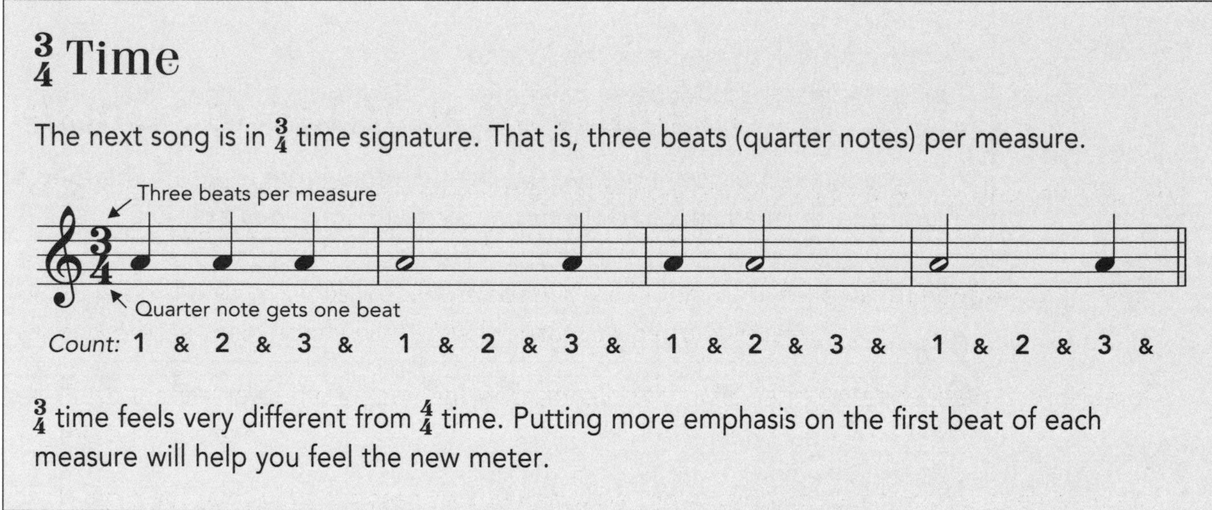

$\frac{3}{4}$ Time

The next song is in $\frac{3}{4}$ time signature. That is, three beats (quarter notes) per measure.

$\frac{3}{4}$ time feels very different from $\frac{4}{4}$ time. Putting more emphasis on the first beat of each measure will help you feel the new meter.

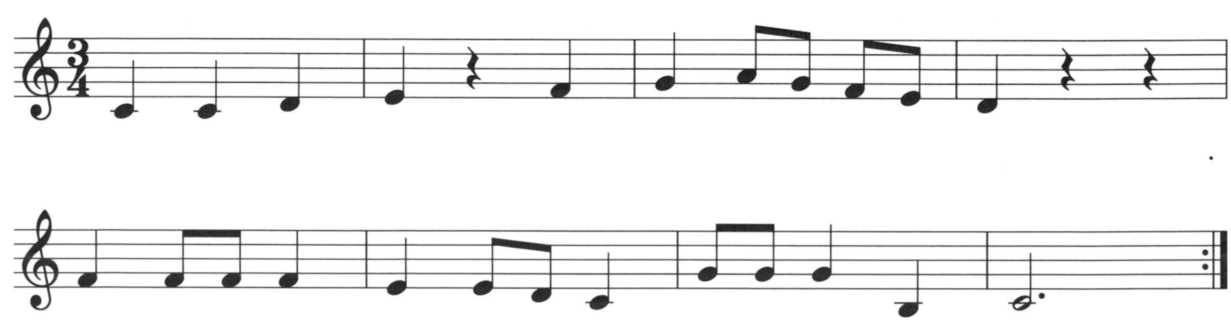

Morning (from Peer Gynt)

Hand and Finger Position

Now is a good time to go back to page 7 and review proper hand and finger position. This is very important to proper technique. Keeping the fingers curved over the valves will allow your fingers and hands to be relaxed and will aid in getting from one note to another quickly, easily, and accurately. Remember to rest the tips of your fingers on the valves and to let your left hand support the weight of the instrument.

- As you finger the notes on your trumpet, you can practice quietly by speaking the names of the notes, counting out the rhythms, or singing or whistling the pitches, or buzzing on the mouthpiece.
- Don't let your cheeks puff out when you play.
- Keep the center section of your lips relaxed at all times.
- Use plenty of air and keep it moving **through** the instrument.

Track 39

Mexican Clapping Song ("Chiapanecas")

Accent

The accent (>) means you should emphasize the note to which it is attached. Do this by using a more explosive "t" on the "tu" with which you produce the note.

Track 40

Hot Muffins (New Note: B♭)

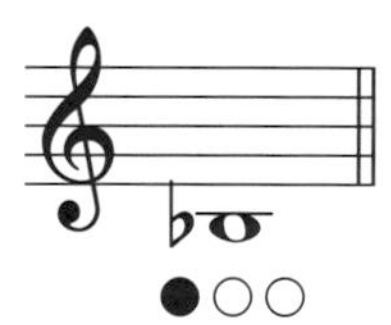

Sharps, Flats, and Naturals

Any sharp (♯), flat (♭), or natural (♮) sign that appears in the music but is not in the key signature is called an **accidental**. The accidental in the next example is an B♭ and it effects all of the B's for the rest of the measure.

A **sharp** (♯) raises the pitch of a note by one half step.

A **flat** (♭) lowers the pitch of a note by one half step.

A **natural** (♮) cancels a previous sharp or flat, returning a note to its original pitch.

When a song requires a note to be a half step higher or lower, you'll see a sharp (♯), flat (♭), or natural (♮) sign in front of it. This tells you to raise or lower the note for that measure only. We'll see more of these "accidentals" as we continue learning more notes on the trumpet.

Cossack Dance

Notice the repeat sign at the end of the fourth measure. Although this particular repeat sign does not occur at the end of the exercise, it behaves just like any other repeat sign. Play the repeated section twice, then continue.

Basic Blues (New Note: B♭)

For higher notes, don't press the mouthpiece hard against your lips. Instead, follow these suggestions:

- Firm the corners of your mouth.
- Raise the back of your tongue slightly, as if whispering "tee."
- Blow the air slightly faster through your instrument.

Track 43

High Flying

Key Signature – F

A **key signature** tells which notes are played as sharps or flats throughout the entire piece. Until now, all of the exercises have been written in the **Key of C**, which has no sharps or flats. This exercise introduces a new key signature: the **Key of F**. Play B♭ throughout the piece.

1st and 2nd Endings

The use of **1st and 2nd endings** is a variant on the basic repeat sign. You play through the music to the repeat sign and repeat as always, but the second time through the music, skip the measure or measures under the "first ending" and go directly to the "second ending."

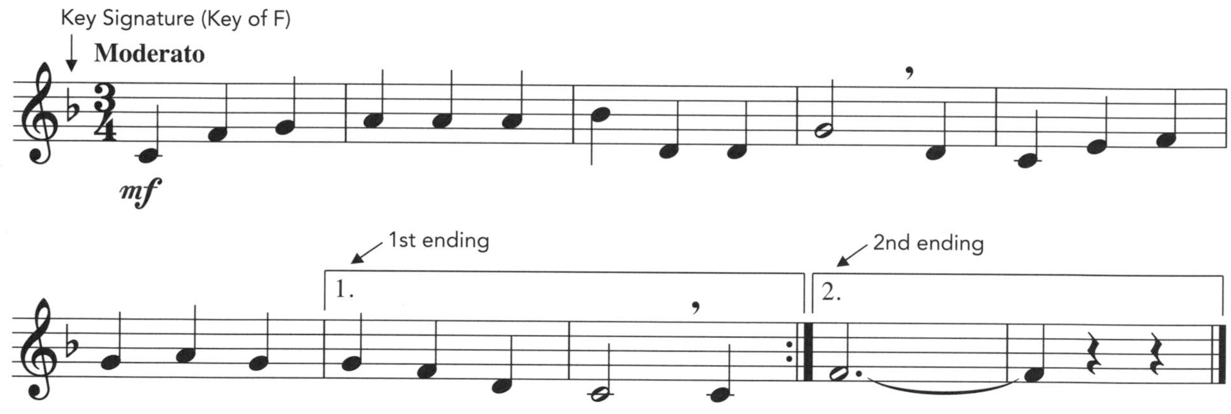

Track 44

Up On A Housetop

Lesson 7

The Big Airstream (New Note: C)

Waltz Theme

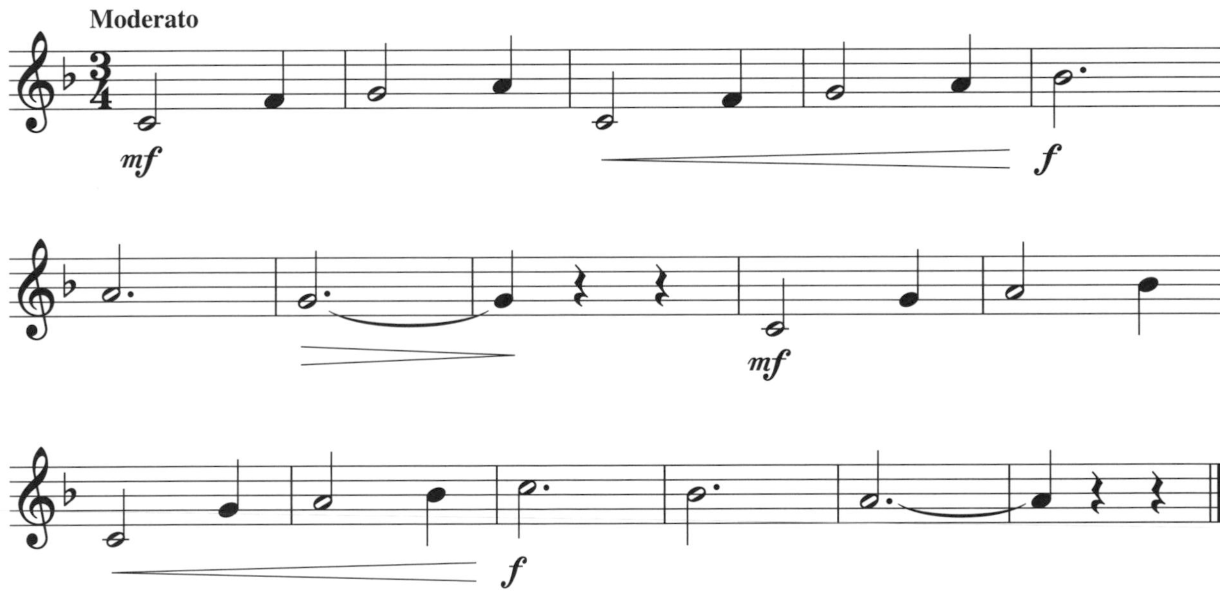

Down By The Station

Track 48

Banana Boat Song

D.C. al Fine

At the **D.C. al Fine**, play again from the beginning, stopping at **Fine**. D.C. is the abbreviation for Da Capo (*dah cah' poh*), which means "to the beginning." Fine (*fee' neh*) means "the end."

Always check the key signature.

Track 49

Razor's Edge (New Note: F♯)

Sharp Sign

A **sharp** sign (♯) raises the pitch of a note by a half-step for the remainder of the measure.

Track 50

The Music Box

Track 51

Smooth Operator

Slur

A curved line connecting notes of different pitch is called a **slur**. Notice the difference between a slur and a tie, which connects notes of the **same** pitch.

Only tongue the first note of a slur. As you finger the next note, keep the breath going.

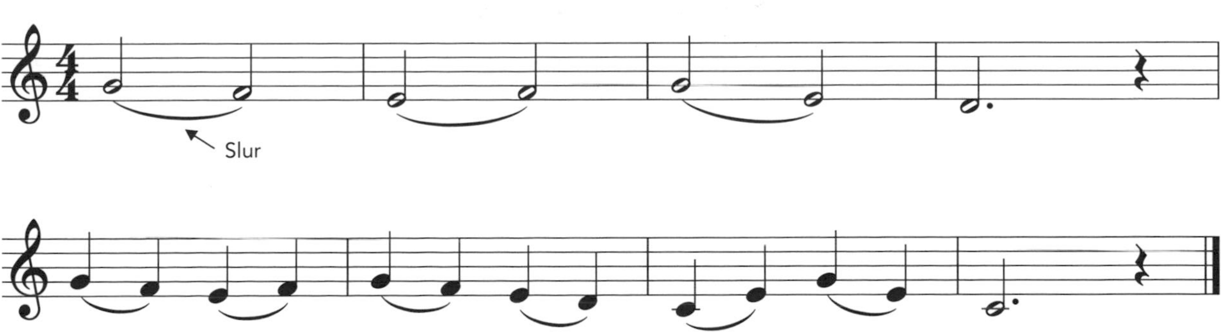

Track 52

Gliding Along

This exercise is almost identical to the previous one. Notice how the different slurs change the tonguing.

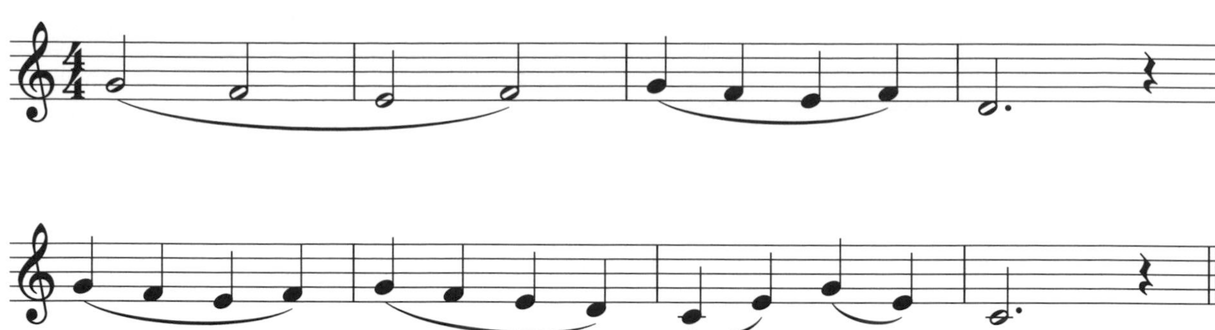

Track 53

Take The Lead (New Note: B)

Track 54

The Cold Wind

Phrase

A phrase is a musical "sentence," often 2 or 4 measures long. Try to play a phrase in one breath.

Track 55

Satin Latin

Key Signature – G

A key signature with one sharp indicates that all written F's should be played as F♯'s. This is the **Key of G**.

Multiple Measure Rest

Sometimes you won't play for several measures. The number above the **multiple measure rest** (⊢⊣) indicates how many full measures to rest. Count through the silent measures.

Track 56

Naturally

Natural Sign

A natural sign (♮) cancels a flat or a sharp for the remainder of the measure.

Track 57

The Flat Zone (New Note: E♭)

Check the key signature.

Track 58

On Top Of Old Smokey

Track 59

All Through The Night

Dotted Quarter Note

Remember that a dot adds half the value of the note. A dotted quarter note followed by a eighth note (♩. ♪) and (♩‿♪♪) have the same rhythmic value.

Track 60

Sea Chanty

Always use a full air stream.

Track 61

Scarborough Fair

Track 62

Auld Lang Syne

Lesson 10

Notes that are slurred without changing the fingering are called **lip slurs**. Brass players practice lip slurs to develop a stronger air stream and embouchure, and to increase range. You should practice lip slurs every day. To play lip slurs well:

- Keep your throat as open and relaxed as possible. If your throat is tense, imagine that you are yawning as you play.
- While playing the first note of a lip slur, think the pitch of the slurred note before you play it.
- Keep the air stream full and steady to the end of the slur. This doesn't mean that you should play loudly, but that you should support the tone with your breath.

Track 63

Slur Exercise No. 1 (Lip Slur)

Track 64

Slur Exercise No. 2

Track 65

Slur Exercise No. 3 (Lip Slur)

Technique Trax

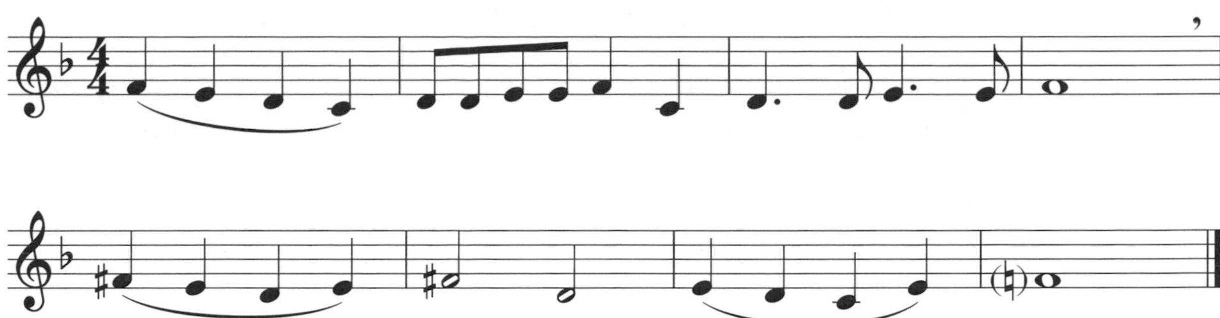

Stepping Stones (New Note: D)

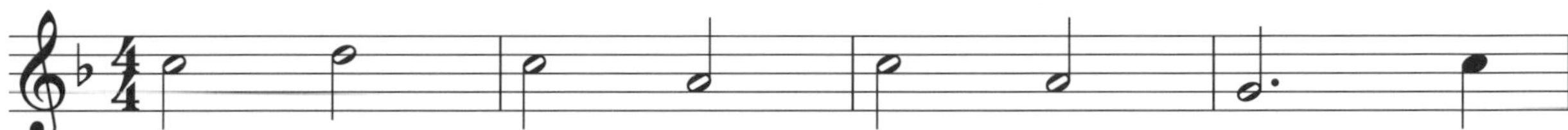

Austrian Waltz

Track 69

Michael Row The Boat Ashore

Repeat the section of music enclosed by the repeat signs (‖: :‖). If 1st and 2nd endings are used, they are played as usual—but go back only to the first repeat sign, not to the beginning.

Track 70

Finlandia

C Time Signature

Common time (C) is the same as $\frac{4}{4}$.

Track 71

When The Saints Go Marching In

Track 72

Botany Bay

Track 73

The Streets Of Laredo

A Quick Review

Posture

Whether sitting on the edge of your chair or standing, you should always keep your:

- Spine straight and tall,
- Shoulders back and relaxed, and
- Feet flat on the floor.

Holding Your Trumpet

- The fingers and thumb of your left hand should be placed around the valves firmly enough to support the trumpet's weight, but keep your hand and arm relaxed. Don't squeeze!
- Rest the fingers of your right hand gently on the valves with your little finger on top of the hook (or ring). Keep your fingers arched comfortably with only the pads of your fingertips touching the valves. You should not hold up your trumpet with your right hand. That will tense up your hand and limit your dexterity.

Taking Care of Your Instrument

- To keep the valves working well, oil them sparingly once or twice a week. Unscrew the cap on top of each valve, lift it part way out, and oil lightly.
- To keep the valve slides working smoothly, pull them out of the instrument one at a time and grease them lightly with slide lubricant or petroleum jelly.
- Flush the inside of the instrument occasionally with lukewarm water to keep the inside of the tubing clean.
- Keep a soft cloth in your case so you can wipe the outside of your trumpet each time you are through playing. If you allow finger marks to remain, you might damage the finish.
- If a slide, valve, or your mouthpiece becomes stuck, get help from your music dealer. Special tools should be used to prevent damage to your instrument.

Warm-ups

Like athletes, musicians need to "warm up" before they perform. A good warm-up will loosen up the muscles of the embouchure and tongue, relax the hands, and focus your mind on playing the instrument. The first three tracks are good warm-up exercises that should be played every day. Before each exercise, take a full and comfortable breath. Work for a smooth, steady tone.

Track 74

Range and Flexibility Builder

Track 75

Technique Trax

Track 76

More Technique Trax

- Be certain that your cheeks don't puff out when you blow.
- Keep the center section of your lips relaxed at all times.
- For higher notes, firm the corners of your mouth slightly.
- Blow enough air through your trumpet to produce a full, even tone but don't "blast."

Track 77

Eighth Note March

Eighth Note/Rest

Recall that an eighth note (♪ or ♪) gets 1/2 of one beat. An equivalent period of silence is represented by an ***eighth rest*** (𝄾).

Track 78

Minuet

Track 79

Eighth Notes Off The Beat

Track 80

Eighth Note Scramble

Track 81

Dancing Melody (New Note: A♭)

Track 82

El Capitan

Ready for a quick lesson in music theory? A ***scale*** is a sequence of notes in ascending or descending order. Like a musical "ladder," each step is the next consecutive note in the key. The scale in the key of C is a specific pattern of ***half steps*** and ***whole steps*** (more on this later) between one C and another C an ***octave*** higher or lower.

The same pattern of half steps and whole steps beginning on a different pitch would produce a different key with a different key signature.

The distance between two pitches is called an ***interval***. Starting with "1" on the lower note, count each line and space between the notes. The number of the higher note is the distance of the interval. A whole step or half step is called a ***second***, the interval between steps 1 and 3 is called a ***third***, and so on. Notice that the interval between scale steps 4 and 6, for example, is also a third.

You already know a sharp raises the pitch of a note. Now you know a sharp raises the pitch of a note by a half-step. Similarly, a flat lowers the pitch of a note one half-step. Two notes that are written differently, but sound the same (and are played with the same fingering) are called enharmonics.

Track 83

Dark Shadows – A♭/G♯

Notice the G♯ in the second full measure (that is, not counting the partial measure with the pick-up note). It is the same pitch and is played with the same fingering as the A♭ in the fourth measure.

Track 84

Notes In Disguise – E♭/D♯

Track 85

Half-Steppin'

Chromatic Scale

At the beginning of this lesson, we saw examples of half steps and whole steps. The smallest distance between two notes is a half-step. A scale made up of consecutive half-steps is called a ***chromatic scale***.

Track 86

March Slav

Largo

Largo *(lahr' goh)* is a tempo indication that means "slow and solemn."

Track 87

Egyptian Dance

Look for the enharmonics.

Track 88

Chroma-Zone

Lesson 14

Notes that aren't slurred should be started with the tongue. To tongue correctly:

- Place the tip of your tongue lightly behind your fron teeth and start each tone as if whispering "tah."
- Make sure your tongue does not project beyond your teeth.
- Start every tone with a neat, clean attack.
- Project your air stream all the way through the trumpet on every note.
- Use your tongue to start a tone but not to stop it: "tah," not "tut."
- Keep your tongue and throat as relaxed as possible at all times.
- Don't move your jaw and lips when tonguing. Check yourself by looking in a mirror as you play.

Track 89

Technique Trax

Track 90

Treading Lightly

Staccato

Staccato *(sta kah' toe)* notes are played lightly and with separation. They are marked with a dot above or below the note. Shorten each note by stopping the air stream.

Track 91

Smooth Move

Tenuto

Tenuto (*tih noo' toe*) notes are played smoothly and connected, holding each note for its full value until the next is played. They are marked with a straight line above or below the note.

Track 92

Shifting Gears

Track 93

Technique Trax

Track 94

Grandfather's Clock

Track 95

Glow Worm

Allegretto, Ritardando

There are two new terms in this exercise. ***Allegretto*** *(ahl ih gret' toh)* is a tempo indication, usually a little slower than Allegro and with a lighter style. ***Ritardando*** *(rih tar dahn' doh)* means the tempo gradually gets slower. It is usually abbreviated ***rit.*** or ***ritard***.

Paul Lincke

Lesson 15

Track 96

Alma Mater (New Note: E)

Always practice long tones on new notes.

Track 97

Loch Lomond

Track 98

Molly Malone

Key Change

The key can change in the middle of a piece. You will usually see a double bar line and a new key signature at the ***key change***. You may also see natural signs reminding you to "cancel" previous sharps and flats.

Track 99

A Cut Above

Alla Breve

Alla Breve *(ah' la bra' ve)*, commonly called ***cut time***, has a time signature of 𝄵 or $\frac{2}{2}$. The top "2" indicates two beats per measure. The bottom "2" means a half note (𝅗𝅥), not a quarter note, gets one beat. Of course, this means a whole note (𝅝) receives two beats and a quarter note (♩) only gets 1/2 beat.

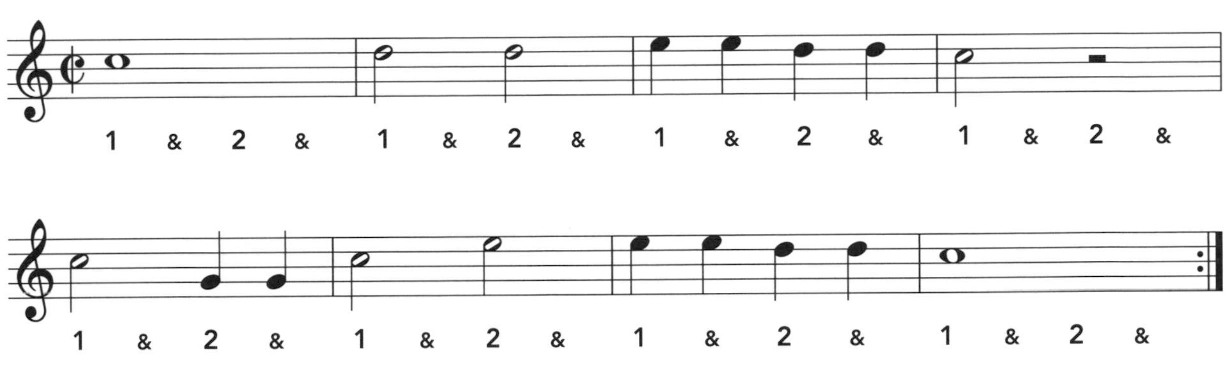

Track 100

Yankee Doodle

First, play the version in $\frac{2}{4}$. Then repeat the track and play the cut time version. Is there any difference?

The Victors

Notice the 𝅗𝅥. ♩ patterns. In cut time, the dotted half note receives 1½ beats and the quarter note receives ½ beat.

Track 102

A-Roving

Mezzo Piano

We have already seen dynamic markings such as ***p***, ***mf***, and ***f***. ***Mezzo piano*** (*met' zo pee ahn' no*), abbreviated ***mp***, means moderately soft: a little louder than piano, not as loud as mezzo forte.

Remember to use a full breath support at all dynamic levels.

Track 103

In Sync

Syncopation

Generally, the notes ***on*** the beat (that's the 1's, 2's, 3's and such) are played a bit stronger or louder than the notes on the ***off-beats*** (that's the &'s). When an accent or emphasis is given to a note that is not normally on a strong beat, it is called ***syncopation***. This sort of "off-beat" feel is common in many popular and classical styles.

Track 104

La Roca

Track 105

You're A Grand Old Flag

Rehearsal Numbers

In longer pieces, the publisher sometimes includes ***rehearsal numbers*** to help the conductor or band leader start and stop the ensemble easily. Sometimes they are letters like A, B, C; sometimes numbers like 1, 2, 3. Frequently, such as here, they are measure numbers.

Crescendo, Decrescendo

A gradual increase in volume is called ***crescendo*** *(kreh shen' doh)*. It is usually indicated by ***cresc.*** or <. A corresponding gradual decrease in volume is called ***decrescendo*** *(deh kre shen' doh)*, abbreviated ***decresc.***, or ***diminuendo*** *(dih meh nyu ehn' doh)*, abbreviated ***dim***. A decrescendo (diminuendo) may be represented by >.

George M. Cohan

Track 106

The Minstrel Boy (New Note: C♯)

This exercise introduces a new key signature: the key of D. Play all F's as F♯, and all C's as C♯.

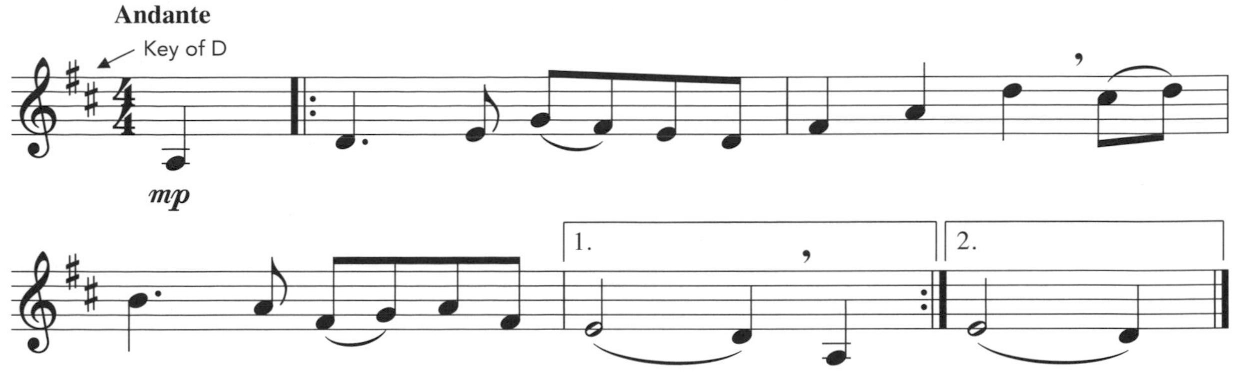

Track 107

Close Call (New Note: C♯)

Track 108

Winning Streak

Pay attention to the syncopation. It is similar to what you played earlier, but now the time signature is ₵.

Track 109

Sixteenth Note Fanfare

Sixteenth Notes

A sixteenth note (♬ or 𝅘𝅥𝅯) has half the value of an eighth note. In $\frac{4}{4}$, $\frac{3}{4}$, or $\frac{2}{4}$ time, four sixteenth notes (♬♬) get one beat.

Track 110

Moving Along

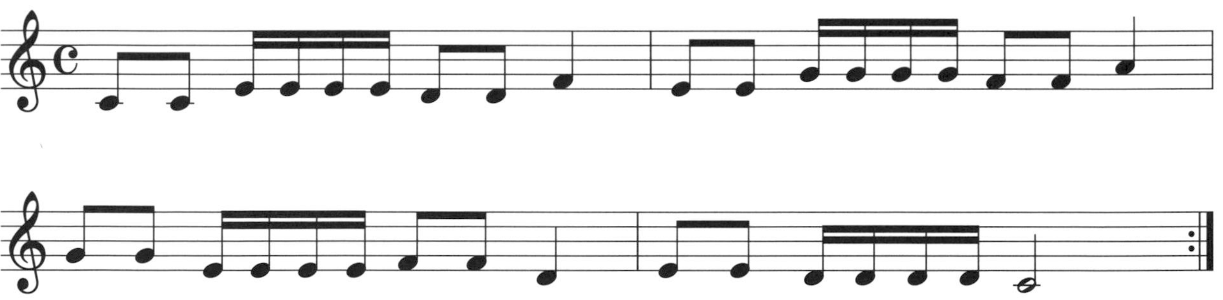

Track 111

Comin' Round The Mountain Variations

Track 112

Sea Chantey

Observe that an eighth note and two sixteenths are normally written ♪♬. This has the same rhythmic pattern as ♪♪♪.

Track 113

American Fanfare (New Note: E♭)

Maestoso

Maestoso *(mah ee stoh' soh)* means "majestic, stately, and dignified."

Track 114

Scale Study

This new key signature indicates the key of B♭. The first four measures consist of the B♭ scale.

Bill Bailey

Moderato

f

17

Lesson 18

Track 116

Rhythm Etude

Observe that two sixteenth notes followed by an eighth are normally written ♬♪. This has the same rhythmic pattern as ♬♬.

Track 117

Celtic Dance

Track 118

The Galway Piper

Track 119

Marching Along

The figures ♩‿♫ and ♩. ♪ are equivalent.

Track 120

S'vivon

Track 121

Toreador Song

Maestoso

mf

5

f

mf

13

f

La Cumparsita (New Note: A♭/G♯)

The Yellow Rose Of Texas

Check the key signature.

Track 124

Scale Study (New Note: F)

As you play higher:

- Move the corners of your mouth slightly inward toward the mouthpiece.
- Increase the speed of the air stream.
- Make the inside of your mouth more narrow or raise the back of your tongue slightly.
- Decrease the size of the opening between your lips.

Track 125

American Patrol

Track 126

Aria (From Marriage Of Figaro)

Track 127

The Stars And Stripes Forever

¢ ♩. ♪ = 2/4 ♪. ♬

John Philip Sousa

March Tempo

f

17

Track 128

Lazy Day

$\frac{6}{8}$ Time

Now you will be introduced to a new time signature: $\frac{6}{8}$. The "6" on top indicates that there are six beats per measure. The "8" on the bottom indicates that the eighth note gets one beat. If the eighth note (♪) gets one beat, then it follows that a dotted quarter note (♩.) receives three beats and a dotted half note (𝅗𝅥.) gets six.

$\frac{6}{8}$ time is usually played with slight emphasis on the 1st and 4th beats of each measure. This divides the measure into two groups of three beats each.

Track 129

Row Your Boat

Track 130

Jolly Good Fellow

Track 131

When Johnny Comes Marching Home

In faster music, the primary beats in $\frac{6}{8}$ time (beats 1 and 4) will make the music feel like it's counted in "2," but with a ***triple subdivision*** of the beat rather than ***duple***.

Enharmonics

Remember that notes which sound the same but have different names are called ***enharmonics***. These are some common enharmonics that you'll use in the exercises below.

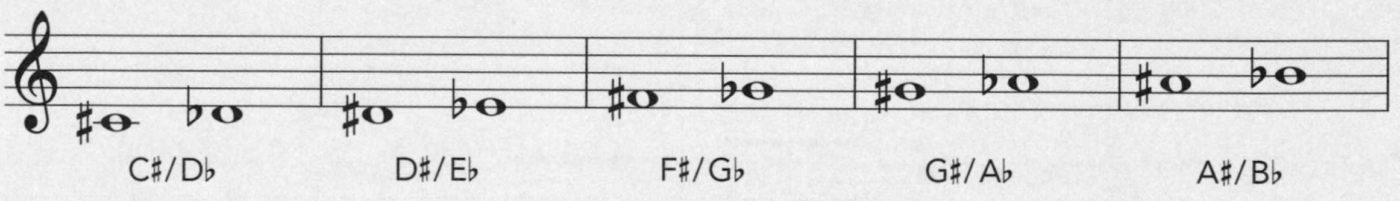

Chromatic passages are usually written using enharmonic notes – sharps when going up and flats when going down.

Track 132

Chromatic Scale

Practice slowly until you are sure of all the fingerings.

Track 133

Technique Trax

Track 134

Staccato Study

Track 135

Yankee Doodle Dandy

George M. Cohan

Track 136

Three To Get Ready

Triplet

A *triplet* is a group of 3 notes played in the time usually occupied by 2. In $\frac{2}{4}$, $\frac{3}{4}$, or $\frac{4}{4}$ time, an eighth note triplet (♪♪♪) is spread evenly across one beat.

Track 137

Triplet Study

Track 138

Theme From Faust

Track 139

Scale Study

New Notes: F♯ G

Track 140

Over The River And Through The Woods

Track 141

On The Move

Higher Ground

Track 143

Doodle All Day

Track 144

D.S. March

D.S. al Fine

Play until you see ***D.S. al Fine***. Then go back to the sign (𝄋) and play until the word ***Fine***. D.S. is the abbreviation for ***Dal Segno*** *(dahl say' nio)*, which is Italian for "from the sign," and Fine *(fee' nay)* means "the end."

Track 145

Tarantella

Track 146

Emperor Waltz

Andantino

Andantino *(ahn dahn tee' noh)* is a tempo between Andante and Moderato.

Track 147

Unfinished Symphony Theme

Legato

Legato *(leh gah' toh)* means to play in a smooth, graceful manner, almost as if everything was slurred.

Track 148

Greensleeves

Trumpet Scales and Arpeggios

Key of C

Trumpet Scales and Arpeggios

Key of F

Trumpet Scales and Arpeggios

Key of G

Trumpet Scales and Arpeggios

Key of B♭

Play all B's as B-flat and all E's as E-flat.

Trumpet Scales and Arpeggios

Key of D

Glossary of Musical Terms

Accent	An Accent mark (>) means you should emphasize the note to which it is attached.
Accidental	Any sharp (♯), flat (♭), or natural (♮) sign that appears in the music but is not in the key signature is called an Accidental.
Alla Breve	Commonly called cut time, has a time signature of 𝄵 or $\frac{2}{2}$.
Allegretto	A tempo indication usually a little slower than Allegro and with a lighter style.
Allegro	Fast tempo.
Andante	Slower "walking" tempo.
Andantino	A tempo between Andante and Moderato.
Arpeggio	An Arpeggio is a "broken" chord whose notes are played individually.
Bass Clef (𝄢)	(F Clef) indicates the position of note names on a music staff: The fourth line in Bass Clef is F.
Bar Lines	Bar Lines divide the music staff into measures.
Beat	The Beat is the pulse of music, and like a heartbeat it should remain very steady. Counting aloud and foot-tapping help maintain a steady beat.
Breath Mark	The Breath Mark (𝄒) indicates a specific place to inhale. Play the proceeding note for the full length then take a deep, quick breath through your mouth.
Chord	When three or more notes are played together, they form a Chord.
Chromatic Notes	Chromatic Notes are altered with sharps, flats and natural signs which are not in the key signature.
Chromatic Scale	The smallest distance between two notes is a half-step, and a scale made up of consecutive half-steps is called a Chromatic Scale.
Common Time	Common Time (𝄴) is the same as $\frac{4}{4}$ time signature.
Crescendo	Play gradually louder. (*cresc.*)
D.C. al Fine	D.C. al Fine means to play again from the beginning, stopping at Fine. D.C. is the abbreviation for Da Capo, or "to the beginning," and Fine means "the end."
D.S. al Fine	Play until you see D.S. al Fine. Then go back to the sign (𝄋) and play until the word Fine. D.S. is the abbreviation for Dal Segno, which is Italian for "from the sign," and Fine means "the end."
Decrescendo	Play gradually softer. (*decresc.*)

Glossary continued

Diminuendo	Same as decrescendo. (*dim.*)
Dotted Half Note	A note three beats long in duration (𝅗𝅥.). A dot adds half the value of the note.
Dotted Quarter Note	A note one and a half beats long in duration (♩.). A dot adds half the value of the note.
Double Bar (‖)	Indicates the end of a piece of music.
Duet	A composition with two different parts played together.
Dynamics	Dynamics indicate how loud or soft to play a passage of music. Remember to use full breath support to control your tone at all dynamic levels.
Eighth Note	An Eighth Note (♪) receives half the value of a quarter note, that is, half a beat. Two or more eighth notes are usually joined together with a beam, like this: ♫
Eighth Rest	Indicates 1/2 beat of silence. (𝄾)
Embouchure	Your mouth's position on the mouthpiece of the instrument.
Enharmonics	Two notes that are written differently, but sound the same (and played with the same fingering) are called Enharmonics.
Fermata	The Fermata (𝄐) indicates that a note (or rest) is held somewhat longer than normal.
1st & 2nd Endings	The use of 1st and 2nd Endings is a variant on the basic repeat sign. You play through the music to the repeat sign and repeat as always, but the second time through the music, skip the measure or measures under the "first ending" and go directly to the "second ending."
Flat (♭)	Lowers the note a half step and remains in effect for the entire measure.
Forte (***f***)	Play loudly.
Half Note	A Half Note (𝅗𝅥) receives two beats. It's equal in length to two quarter notes.
Half Rest	The Half Rest (𝄼) marks two beats of silence.
Harmony	Two or more notes played together.
Interval	The distance between two pitches is an Interval.
Key Change	When a song changes key you will usually see a double bar line and the new key signature at the key change. You may also see natural signs reminding you to "cancel" previous sharps and flats.
Key Signature	A Key Signature (the group of sharps or flats before the time signature) tells which notes are played as sharps or flats throughout the entire piece.
Largo	Play very slow.

Ledger Lines	Ledger Lines extend the music staff. Notes on ledger lines can be above or below the staff.
Legato	Legato means to play in a smooth, graceful manner, almost as if everything was slurred.
Mezzo Forte (*mf*)	Play moderately loud.
Mezzo Piano (*mp*)	Play moderately soft.
Moderato	Medium or moderate tempo.
Multiple Measure Rest	The number above the staff tells you how many full measures to rest. Count each measure of rest in sequence. (▬)
Music Staff	The Music Staff has 5 lines and 4 spaces where notes and rests are written.
Natural Sign (♮)	Cancels a flat (♭) or sharp (♯) and remains in effect for the entire measure.
Notes	Notes tell us how high or low to play by their placement on a line or space of the music staff, and how long to play by their shape.
Phrase	A Phrase is a musical "sentence," often 2 or 4 measures long.
Piano (*p*)	Play soft.
Pitch	The highness or lowness of a note which is indicated by the horizontal placement of the note on the music staff.
Pick-Up Notes	One or more notes that come before the first full measure. The beats of Pick-Up Notes are subtracted from the last measure.
Quarter Note	A Quarter Note (♩) receives one beat. There are 4 quarter notes in a $\frac{4}{4}$ measure.
Quarter Rest	The Quarter Rest (𝄽) marks one beat of silence.
Repeat Sign	The Repeat Sign (:‖) means to play once again from the beginning without pause. Repeat the section of music enclosed by the repeat signs (‖: :‖). If 1st and 2nd endings are used, they are played as usual—but go back only to the first repeat sign, not to the beginning.
Rests	Rests tell us to count silent beats.
Rhythm	Rhythm refers to how long, or for how many beats a note lasts.
Ritardando (*rit.*)	Means the tempo gradually gets slower.
Scale	A Scale is a sequence of notes in ascending or descending order. Like a musical "ladder," each step is the next consecutive note in the key signature.
Sharp (♯)	Raises the note a half step and remains in effect for the entire measure.

Glossary continued

Sixteenth Note — A sixteenth note (𝅘𝅥𝅯 or 𝅘𝅥𝅯) has half the value of an eighth note. In $\frac{4}{4}$, $\frac{3}{4}$, or $\frac{2}{4}$ time, four sixteenth notes (♬♬) get one beat.

Slur — A curved line connecting notes of different pitch is called a Slur.

Staccato — Play the notes lightly and with separation.

Tempo — Tempo is the speed of music.

Tempo Markings — Tempo Markings are usually written above the staff, in Italian. (Allegro, Moderato, Andante)

Tenuto — Play the notes smoothly and connected, holding each note for its full value until the next is played.

Tie — A Tie is a curved line connecting two notes of the same pitch. It indicates that instead of playing both notes, you play the first note and hold it for the total time value of both notes.

Time Signature — Indicates how many beats per measure and what kind of note gets one beat.

Treble Clef (𝄞) — (G Clef) indicates the position of note names on a music staff: The second line in Treble Clef is G.

Trio — A Trio is a composition with three parts played together.

Triplet — A triplet is a group of three notes played in the time usually occupied by two. In $\frac{2}{4}$, $\frac{3}{4}$, or $\frac{4}{4}$ time, an eighth note triplet (♫♪ with 3) is spread evenly across one beat.

Whole Note — A Whole Note (𝅝) lasts for four full beats (a complete measure in $\frac{4}{4}$ time).

Whole Rest — The Whole Rest (-) indicates a whole measure of silence.

Fingering Chart for Trumpet

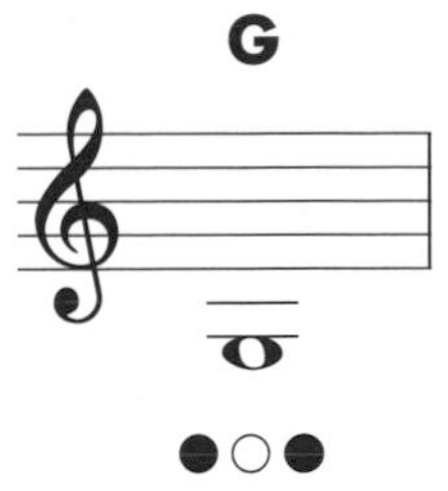

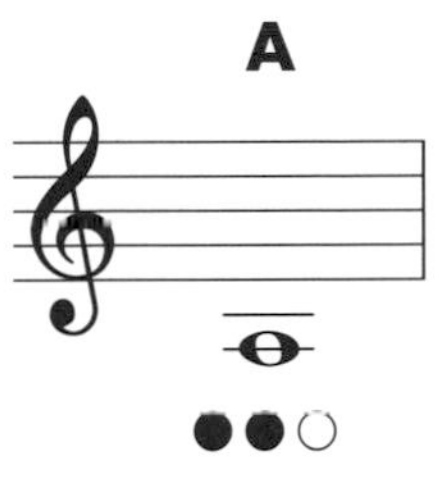

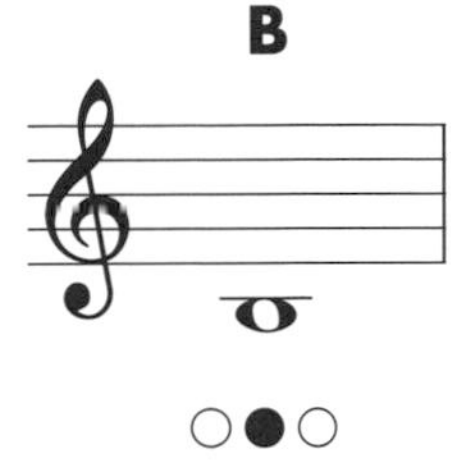

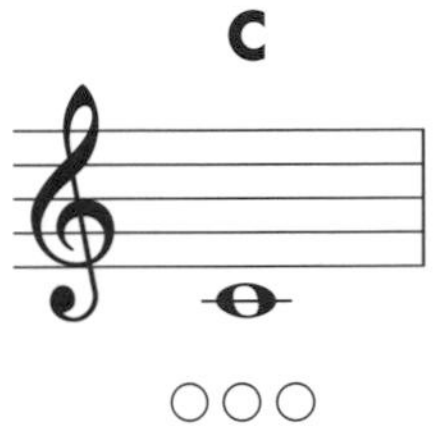

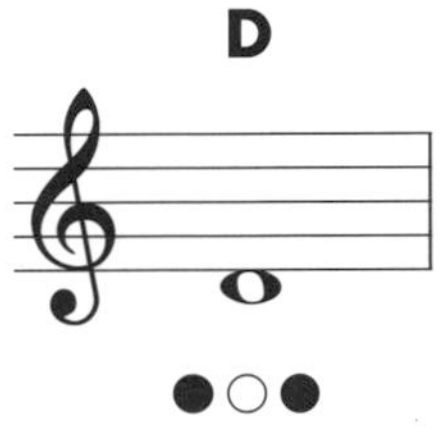

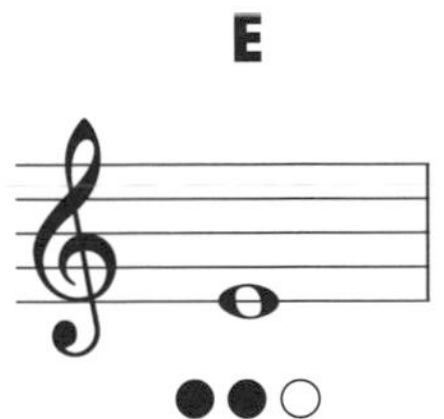

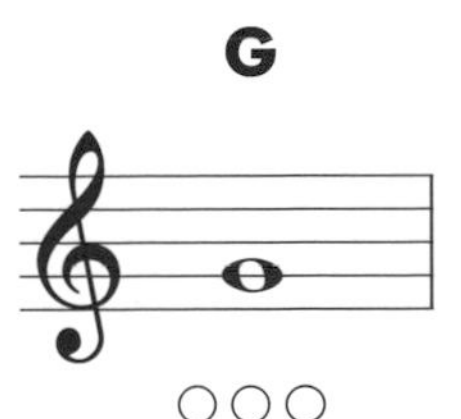

Fingering Chart for Trumpet

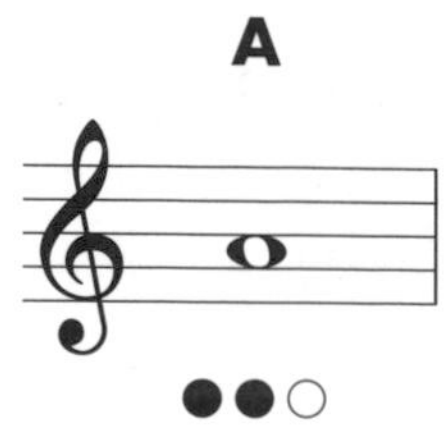

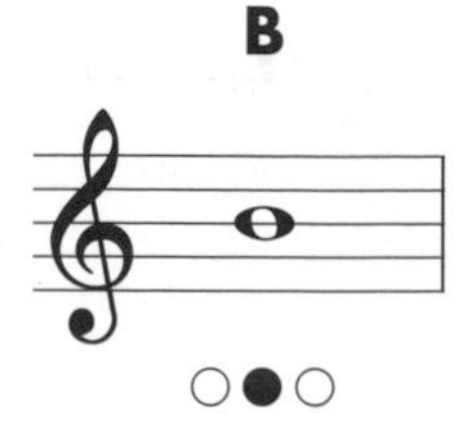

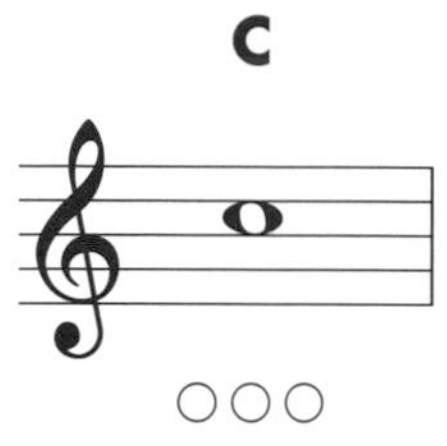

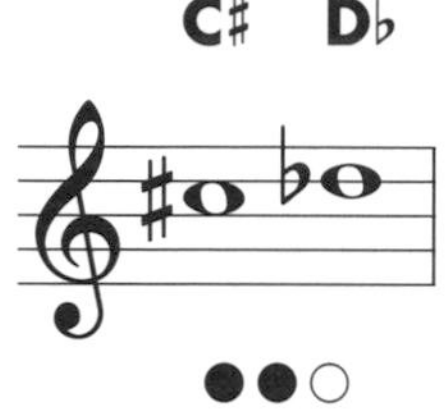

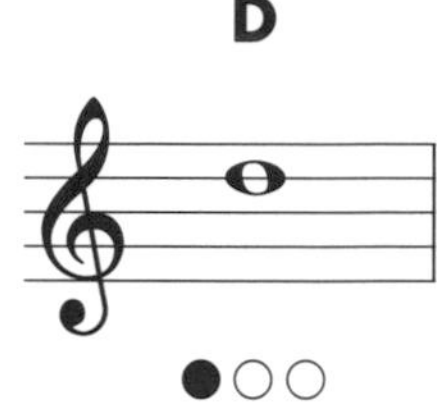

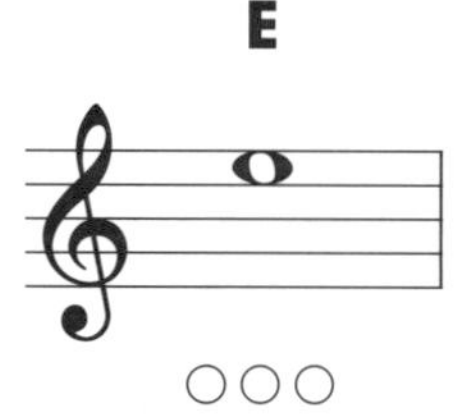

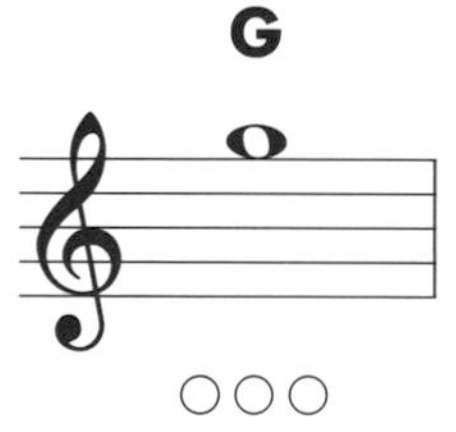

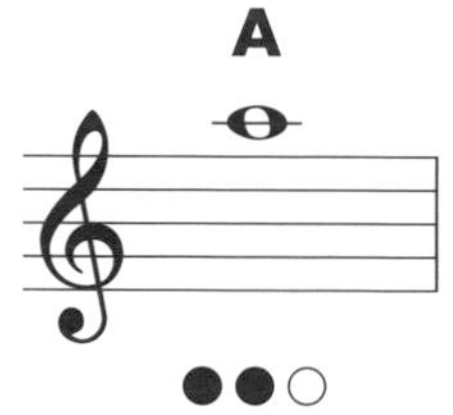

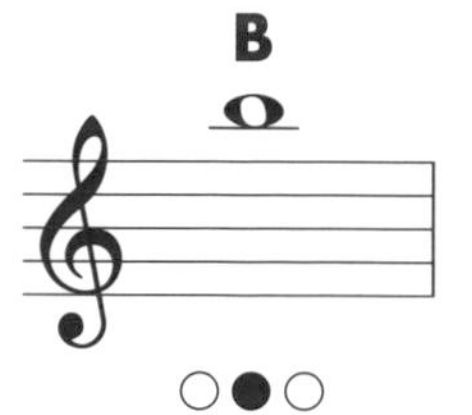

Play Today! Series

The Ultimate Self-Teaching Series

These are complete guides to the basics, designed to offer quality instruction, terrific songs, and professional-quality audio with tons of full-demo tracks and instruction. Each book includes over 70 great songs and examples!

Play Accordion Today!
00701744 Level 1 Book/Audio $10.99
00702657 Level 1 Songbook Book/Audio $12.99

Play Alto Sax Today!
00842049 Level 1 Book/Audio $9.99
00842050 Level 2 Book/Audio $9.99
00320359 DVD $14.95
00842051 Songbook Book/Audio $12.95
00699555 Beginner's – Level 1 Book/Audio & DVD $19.95
00699492 Play Today Plus Book/Audio ... $14.95

Play Banjo Today!
00699897 Level 1 Book/Audio $9.99
00701006 Level 2 Book/Audio $9.99
00320913 DVD $14.99
00115999 Songbook Book/Audio $12.99
00701873 Beginner's – Level 1 Book/Audio & DVD $19.95

Play Bass Today!
00842020 Level 1 Book/Audio $9.99
00842036 Level 2 Book/Audio $9.99
00320356 DVD $14.95
00842037 Songbook Book/Audio $12.95
00699552 Beginner's – Level 1 Book/Audio & DVD $19.99

Play Cello Today!
00151353 Level 1 Book/Audio $9.99

Play Clarinet Today!
00842046 Level 1 Book/Audio $9.99
00842047 Level 2 Book/Audio $9.99
00320358 DVD $14.95
00842048 Songbook Book/Audio $12.95
00699554 Beginner's – Level 1 Book/Audio & DVD $19.95
00699490 Play Today Plus Book/Audio ... $14.95

Play Dobro Today!
00701505 Level 1 Book/Audio $9.99

Play Drums Today!
00842021 Level 1 Book/Audio $9.99
00842038 Level 2 Book/Audio $9.95
00320355 DVD $14.95
00842039 Songbook Book/Audio $12.95
00699551 Beginner's – Level 1 Book/Audio & DVD $19.95
00703291 Starter $24.99

Play Flute Today
00842043 Level 1 Book/Audio $9.95
00842044 Level 2 Book/Audio $9.99
00320360 DVD $14.95
00842045 Songbook Book/Audio $12.95
00699553 Beginner's – Level 1 Book/Audio & DVD $19.95

Play Guitar Today!
00696100 Level 1 Book/Audio $9.99
00696101 Level 2 Book/Audio $9.99
00320353 DVD $14.95
00696102 Songbook Book/Audio $12.99
00699544 Beginner's – Level 1 Book/Audio & DVD $19.95
00702431 Worship Songbook Book/Audio $12.99
00695662 Complete Kit $29.95

Play Harmonica Today!
00700179 Level 1 Book/Audio $9.99
00320653 DVD $14.99
00701875 Beginner's – Level 1 Book/Audio & DVD $19.95

Play Mandolin Today!
00699911 Level 1 Book/Audio $9.99
00320909 DVD $14.99
00115029 Songbook Book/Audio $12.99
00701874 Beginner's – Level 1 Book/Audio & DVD $19.99

Play Piano Today! Revised Edition
00842019 Level 1 Book/Audio $9.99
00298773 Level 2 Book/Audio $9.95
00842041 Songbook Book/Audio $12.95
00699545 Beginner's – Level 1 Book/Audio & DVD $19.95
00702415 Worship Songbook Book/Audio $12.99
00703707 Complete Kit $22.99

Play Recorder Today!
00700919 Level 1 Book/Audio $7.99
00119830 Complete Kit $19.99

Sing Today!
00699761 Level 1 Book/Audio $10.99

Play Trombone Today!
00699917 Level 1 Book/Audio $12.99
00320508 DVD $14.95

Play Trumpet Today!
00842052 Level 1 Book/Audio $9.99
00842053 Level 2 Book/Audio $9.95
00320357 DVD $14.95
00842054 Songbook Book/Audio $12.95
00699556 Beginner's – Level 1 Book/Audio & DVD $19.95

Play Ukulele Today!
00699638 Level 1 Book/Audio $10.99
00699655 Play Today Plus Book/Audio $9.99
00320985 DVD $14.99
00701872 Beginner's – Level 1 Book/Audio & DVD $19.95
00650743 Book/Audio/DVD with Ukulele $39.99
00701002 Level 2 Book/Audio $9.99
00702484 Level 2 Songbook Book/Audio $12.99
00703290 Starter $24.99

Play Viola Today!
00142679 Level 1 Book/Audio $9.99

Play Violin Today!
00699748 Level 1 Book/Audio $9.99
00701320 Level 2 Book/Audio $9.99
00321076 DVD $14.99
00701700 Songbook Book/Audio $12.99
00701876 Beginner's – Level 1 Book/Audio & DVD $19.95

www.halleonard.com

Prices, contents and availability subject to change without notice.

0719
102

HAL•LEONARD®

TRUMPET PLAY-ALONG

The Trumpet Play-Along Series will help you play your favorite songs quickly and easily. Just follow the printed music, listen to the sound-alike recordings and hear how the trumpet should sound, and then play along using the separate backing tracks.

1. POPULAR HITS

Copacabana (At the Copa) (Barry Manilow) • Does Anybody Really Know What Time It Is? (Chicago) • Hot Hot Hot (Buster Poindexter) • Livin' La Vida Loca (Ricky Martin) • Ring of Fire (Johnny Cash) • Sir Duke (Stevie Wonder) • Sussudio (Phil Collins) • Will It Go Round in Circles (Billy Preston).

00137383 Book/Online Audio $16.99

2. TRUMPET CLASSICS

Ciribiribin (Harry James) • Feels So Good (Chuck Mangione) • Java (Al Hirt) • Music to Watch Girls By (Bob Crewe Generation) • Spanish Flea (Herb Alpert) • Sugar Blues (Al Hirt) • A Taste of Honey (Herb Alpert) • The Toy Trumpet (Raymond Scott).

00137384 Book/Online Audio $16.99

3. CLASSIC ROCK

All You Need Is Love (The Beatles) • Deacon Blues (Steely Dan) • Feelin' Stronger Every Day (Chicago) • Higher Love (Steve Winwood) • September (Earth, Wind & Fire) • Spinning Wheel (Blood, Sweat & Tears) • 25 or 6 to 4 (Chicago) • Vehicle (Ides of March).

00137385 Book/Online Audio $16.99

4. GREAT THEMES

Cherry Pink and Apple Blossom White (Perez Prado) • Deborah's Theme (Ennio Morricone) • Dragnet (Walter Schumann) • The Godfather Waltz (Nino Rota) • Gonna Fly Now (Bill Conti) • Green Hornet Theme (Al Hirt) • The Odd Couple (Neal Hefti) • Sugar Lips (Al Hirt).

00137386 Book/Online Audio $16.99

6. MILES DAVIS

Airegin • Bye Bye Blackbird • Doxy • E.S.P. • Half Nelson • Move • So What • Summertime.

00137447 Book/Online Audio $16.99

7. JAZZ BALLADS

Body and Soul • Easy Living • Everything Happens to Me • I Remember Clifford • Over the Rainbow • Stella by Starlight • They Can't Take That Away from Me • Where or When.

00137475 Book/Online Audio $16.99

www.halleonard.com

Prices, contents, and availability subject to change without notice.

1217

HAL•LEONARD INSTRUMENTAL PLAY-ALONG

Your favorite songs are arranged just for solo instrumentalists with this outstanding series. Each book includes great full-accompaniment play-along audio so you can sound just like a pro! Check out **www.halleonard.com** to see all the titles available.

The Beatles

All You Need Is Love • Blackbird • Day Tripper • Eleanor Rigby • Get Back • Here, There and Everywhere • Hey Jude • I Will • Let It Be • Lucy in the Sky with Diamonds • Ob La Di, Ob-La-Da • Penny Lane • Something • Ticket to Ride • Yesterday.

_____00225330 Flute $14.99
_____00225331 Clarinet $14.99
_____00225332 Alto Sax $14.99
_____00225333 Tenor Sax $14.99
_____00225334 Trumpet. $14.99
_____00225335 Horn $14.99
_____00225336 Trombone $14.99
_____00225337 Violin. $14.99
_____00225338 Viola $14.99
_____00225339 Cello $14.99

Chart Hits

All About That Bass • All of Me • Happy • Radioactive • Roar • Say Something • Shake It Off • A Sky Full of Stars • Someone like You • Stay with Me • Thinking Out Loud • Uptown Funk.

_____00146207 Flute $12.99
_____00146208 Clarinet $12.99
_____00146209 Alto Sax $12.99
_____00146210 Tenor Sax $12.99
_____00146211 Trumpet. $12.99
_____00146212 Horn $12.99
_____00146213 Trombone $12.99
_____00146214 Violin. $12.99
_____00146215 Viola $12.99
_____00146216 Cello $12.99

Disney Greats

Arabian Nights • Hawaiian Roller Coaster Ride • It's a Small World • Look Through My Eyes • Yo Ho (A Pirate's Life for Me) • and more.

_____00841934 Flute $12.99
_____00841935 Clarinet $12.99
_____00841936 Alto Sax $12.99
_____00841937 Tenor Sax $12.95
_____00841938 Trumpet. $12.99
_____00841939 Horn $12.99
_____00841940 Trombone $12.99
_____00841941 Violin. $12.99
_____00841942 Viola $12.99
_____00841943 Cello $12.99
_____00842078 Oboe $12.99

The Greatest Showman

Come Alive • From Now On • The Greatest Show • A Million Dreams • Never Enough • The Other Side • Rewrite the Stars • This Is Me • Tightrope.

_____00277389 Flute $14.99
_____00277390 Clarinet $14.99
_____00277391 Alto Sax $14.99
_____00277392 Tenor Sax $14.99
_____00277393 Trumpet. $14.99
_____00277394 Horn $14.99
_____00277395 Trombone $14.99
_____00277396 Violin. $14.99
_____00277397 Viola $14.99
_____00277398 Cello $14.99

Movie and TV Music

The Avengers • Doctor Who XI • Downton Abbey • Game of Thrones • Guardians of the Galaxy • Hawaii Five-O • Married Life • Rey's Theme (from *Star Wars: The Force Awakens*) • The X-Files • and more.

_____00261807 Flute $12.99
_____00261808 Clarinet $12.99
_____00261809 Alto Sax $12.99
_____00261810 Tenor Sax $12.99
_____00261811 Trumpet. $12.99
_____00261812 Horn $12.99
_____00261813 Trombone $12.99
_____00261814 Violin. $12.99
_____00261815 Viola $12.99
_____00261816 Cello $12.99

12 Pop Hits

Believer • Can't Stop the Feeling • Despacito • It Ain't Me • Look What You Made Me Do • Million Reasons • Perfect • Send My Love (To Your New Lover) • Shape of You • Slow Hands • Too Good at Goodbyes • What About Us.

_____00261790 Flute $12.99
_____00261791 Clarinet $12.99
_____00261792 Alto Sax $12.99
_____00261793 Tenor Sax $12.99
_____00261794 Trumpet. $12.99
_____00261795 Horn $12.99
_____00261796 Trombone $12.99
_____00261797 Violin. $12.99
_____00261798 Viola $12.99
_____00261799 Cello $12.99

Songs from Frozen, Tangled and Enchanted

Do You Want to Build a Snowman? • For the First Time in Forever • Happy Working Song • I See the Light • In Summer • Let It Go • Mother Knows Best • That's How You Know • True Love's First Kiss • When Will My Life Begin • and more.

_____00126921 Flute $14.99
_____00126922 Clarinet $14.99
_____00126923 Alto Sax $14.99
_____00126924 Tenor Sax $14.99
_____00126925 Trumpet. $14.99
_____00126926 Horn $14.99
_____00126927 Trombone $14.99
_____00126928 Violin. $14.99
_____00126929 Viola $14.99
_____00126930 Cello $14.99

Top Hits

Adventure of a Lifetime • Budapest • Die a Happy Man • Ex's & Oh's • Fight Song • Hello • Let It Go • Love Yourself • One Call Away • Pillowtalk • Stitches • Writing's on the Wall.

_____00171073 Flute $12.99
_____00171074 Clarinet $12.99
_____00171075 Alto Sax $12.99
_____00171106 Tenor Sax $12.99
_____00171107 Trumpet. $12.99
_____00171108 Horn $12.99
_____00171109 Trombone $12.99
_____00171110 Violin. $12.99
_____00171111 Viola $12.99
_____00171112 Cello $12.99

Wicked

As Long As You're Mine • Dancing Through Life • Defying Gravity • For Good • I'm Not That Girl • Popular • The Wizard and I • and more.

_____00842236 Flute $12.99
_____00842237 Clarinet $12.99
_____00842238 Alto Saxophone $12.99
_____00842239 Tenor Saxophone. $11.95
_____00842240 Trumpet. $12.99
_____00842241 Horn $12.99
_____00842242 Trombone $12.99
_____00842243 Violin. $12.99
_____00842244 Viola $12.99
_____00842245 Cello $12.99

HAL•LEONARD®

101 SONGS

BIG COLLECTIONS OF FAVORITE SONGS ARRANGED FOR SOLO INSTRUMENTALISTS.

101 BROADWAY SONGS

00154199	Flute	$14.99
00154200	Clarinet	$14.99
00154201	Alto Sax	$14.99
00154202	Tenor Sax	$14.99
00154203	Trumpet	$14.99
00154204	Horn	$14.99
00154205	Trombone	$14.99
00154206	Violin	$14.99
00154207	Viola	$14.99
00154208	Cello	$14.99

101 CHRISTMAS SONGS

00278637	Flute	$14.99
00278638	Clarinet	$14.99
00278639	Alto Sax	$14.99
00278640	Tenor Sax	$14.99
00278641	Trumpet	$14.99
00278642	Horn	$14.99
00278643	Trombone	$14.99
00278644	Violin	$14.99
00278645	Viola	$14.99
00278646	Cello	$14.99

101 CLASSICAL THEMES

00155315	Flute	$14.99
00155317	Clarinet	$14.99
00155318	Alto Sax	$14.99
00155319	Tenor Sax	$14.99
00155320	Trumpet	$14.99
00155321	Horn	$14.99
00155322	Trombone	$14.99
00155323	Violin	$14.99
00155324	Viola	$14.99
00155325	Cello	$14.99

101 DISNEY SONGS

00244104	Flute	$16.99
00244106	Clarinet	$16.99
00244107	Alto Sax	$16.99
00244108	Tenor Sax	$16.99
00244109	Trumpet	$16.99
00244112	Horn	$16.99
00244120	Trombone	$16.99
00244121	Violin	$16.99
00244125	Viola	$16.99
00244126	Cello	$16.99

101 HIT SONGS

00194561	Flute	$16.99
00197182	Clarinet	$16.99
00197183	Alto Sax	$16.99
00197184	Tenor Sax	$16.99
00197185	Trumpet	$16.99
00197186	Horn	$16.99
00197187	Trombone	$16.99
00197188	Violin	$16.99
00197189	Viola	$16.99
00197190	Cello	$16.99

101 JAZZ SONGS

00146363	Flute	$14.99
00146364	Clarinet	$14.99
00146366	Alto Sax	$14.99
00146367	Tenor Sax	$14.99
00146368	Trumpet	$14.99
00146369	Horn	$14.99
00146370	Trombone	$14.99
00146371	Violin	$14.99
00146372	Viola	$14.99
00146373	Cello	$14.99

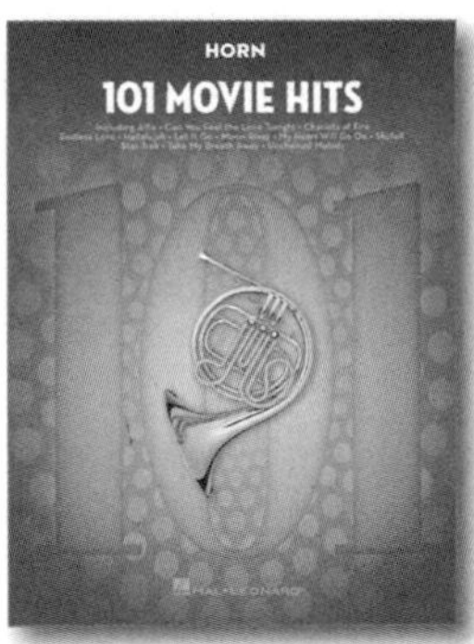

101 MOVIE HITS

00158087	Flute	$14.99
00158088	Clarinet	$14.99
00158089	Alto Sax	$14.99
00158090	Tenor Sax	$14.99
00158091	Trumpet	$14.99
00158092	Horn	$14.99
00158093	Trombone	$14.99
00158094	Violin	$14.99
00158095	Viola	$14.99
00158096	Cello	$14.99

101 POPULAR SONGS

00224722	Flute	$16.99
00224723	Clarinet	$16.99
00224724	Alto Sax	$16.99
00224725	Tenor Sax	$16.99
00224726	Trumpet	$16.99
00224727	Horn	$16.99
00224728	Trombone	$16.99
00224729	Violin	$16.99
00224730	Viola	$16.99
00224731	Cello	$16.99

www.halleonard.com

Prices, contents and availability subject to change without notice.